hamlyn cookery club

Cakes
and bakes

hamlyn cookery club

Cakes
and bakes

First published in 2000 by Hamlyn
an imprint of Octopus Publishing Group Ltd
2–4 Heron Quays
London E14 4JP

British Library Cataloguing-in-Publication Data
A catalogue record for this book is available from the British Library.

ISBN 0 600 599 906

Printed in China

Copy Editor: Heather Thomas
Creative Director: Keith Martin
Design Manager: Bryan Dunn
Designer: Glyn Bridgewater
Jacket Photography: Sean Myers
Picture Researcher: Christine Junemann
Production Controller: Clare Smedley

Notes

1 Both metric and imperial measurements have been given in all recipes. Use one set of measurements only and not a mixture of both.
2 Standard level spoon measurements are used in all recipes.
1 tablespoon = one 15 ml spoon
1 teaspoon = one 5 ml spoon
3 Eggs should be medium unless otherwise stated. The Department of Health advises that eggs should not be consumed raw. This book may contain dishes made with raw or lightly cooked eggs. It is prudent for more vulnerable people such as pregnant or nursing mothers, the elderly, babies and young children to avoid these dishes. Once prepared, these dishes should be refrigerated and eaten promptly.
4 Milk should be full fat unless otherwise stated.
5 Ovens should be preheated to the specified temperature – if using a fan-assisted oven, follow the manufacturer's instructions for adjusting the time and temperature.
6 Measurements for canned food have been given as a standard metric equivalent.

Contents

Introduction

Home baking is very satisfying and there's nothing to compare with the aroma of freshly baked cakes just out of the oven. Your efforts will always be appreciated by your family and friends, so use this inspirational book to get baking!

EQUIPMENT

Before you start baking, it's important to have all the basic equipment ready. For most of the recipes in this book, you will need the following:

• **Basic equipment:** mixing bowls (in various sizes), a measuring jug and set of measuring spoons, a sieve, a spatula and palette knife and a grater.

• **Beating the mixture:** a balloon whisk or wooden spoon or, if you prefer, an electric whisk, a food processor or food mixer.

• **Cake tins:** it is useful to have a selection of these, including sandwich tins in different widths, deeper round or square tins, a Swiss roll tin, a springform cake tin, a muffin pan and a wire rack for cooling cakes. For lining the tins, you will need greaseproof paper and nonstick baking paper.

• **Decorating the cake:** paper and nylon piping bags and a selection of nozzles, silver cake boards and a rolling pin (for rolling out icing and marzipan).

RAISING AGENTS

The main ingredients for baking are flour, butter and eggs, but most cakes also need a raising agent to help them rise. Many recipes specify self-raising flour which already contains some baking powder but others recommend using plain flour mixed with either baking powder, bicarbonate of soda or cream of tartar. Keep these handy in your store cupboard.

SUCCESSFUL BAKING TIPS

For the best results, always follow these simple guidelines:

• Make sure that all the ingredients are at room temperature before you start baking.

• Always preheat the oven to the correct temperature before putting in the cake.

• If using a fan oven, adjust the temperature according to the manufacturer's instruction handbook.

• Use either metric or imperial measures – never both – within one recipe.

- Prepare the baking tin as directed before starting to make the cake.
- Add a little sieved flour with each egg to prevent the mixture curdling.

LINING TINS

You can prevent the cake sticking to the tin by greasing the tin with a little butter, margarine or oil and then flouring lightly, or lining it with greaseproof paper or nonstick baking paper. Trace the outline of the base of the tin onto the lining paper and then cut out the shape of the base. Cut out long strips of paper to line the sides of the tin.

TESTING CAKES

When a cake is cooked, it should be well risen and starting to shrink away from the sides of the tin. If it is a sponge it will look golden. When pressed lightly with a finger, it should spring back. In addition, you can insert a fine metal skewer or the thin blade of a knife into the centre. If it comes out clean, then the cake is cooked. Otherwise, replace it in the oven and bake for a further 5 minutes before retesting.

STORING CAKES

After cooling thoroughly on a wire rack, cakes can be stored in sealed containers or tins. Light sponges will keep well for a couple of days, whereas rich fruit cakes can be wrapped in greaseproof paper or foil and stored successfully for several weeks. If cream or fresh fruit are added to a cake, then it should be kept in the refrigerator.

DECORATING CAKES

How you choose to decorate a cake can be as formal or casual as you wish. Sponge and sandwich cakes can be filled with jam, buttercream or whipped cream and fruit, then simply dusted with caster sugar or sifted icing sugar. More elaborate cakes and gâteaux can be iced or covered with buttercream, frosting or whipped cream.

- Decorating the sides: you can press chopped nuts, flaked almonds or grated chocolate onto the sides of a cake coated with buttercream or cream.
- Decorating the top: you can pipe rosettes of buttercream or cream on top of the cake or use a variety of edible decorations, including candied and glacé fruits, crystallized ginger, angelica and flowers (e.g. rose petals and violets), whole nuts, chocolate curls, citron peel, fresh fruit and moulded icing shapes or marzipan.

As you turn the pages of this book, you will find lots of exciting ideas for cake decorations.

Everyday Cakes

Victoria Sandwich

If you are using two 18 cm (7 inch) tins instead of 20 cm (8 inch) sandwich tins, use 125 g (4 oz) of the main ingredients and 2 eggs. As an alternative filling, arrange a layer of drained mandarin orange segments from a 325 g (11 oz) can between the lemon curd and buttercream. Do not take the mandarin segments quite to the edge of the cake. Other suggestions include sandwiching the cake with just buttercream, or using fresh whipped cream and some sliced strawberries. Decorate the top of the cake by piping with rosettes of cream.

175 g (6 oz) butter, softened
175 g (6 oz) caster sugar
3 eggs
175 g (6 oz) self-raising flour, sifted
a few drops of vanilla essence
1 tablespoon cold water
jellied lemon slices, to decorate
Filling:
175–250 g (6–8 oz) lemon curd
¾ recipe quantity lemon buttercream (see opposite)
caster or icing sugar, for sprinkling

Grease and base line two 20 cm (8 inch) sandwich tins. Beat the butter until soft, then beat in the sugar until light, fluffy and pale in colour.

Beat in the eggs, one at a time, with 1 tablespoon flour to prevent curdling. Fold in the remaining flour, vanilla essence and water. Divide the mixture between the prepared tins and level the tops.

Bake in a preheated oven, 190°C (375°F), Gas Mark 5, for 20–25 minutes until well risen and just firm to the touch. Cool on a wire tray and peel off the paper.

Spread one of the cakes with lemon curd, then cover with two-thirds of the buttercream. Sandwich together and sprinkle with sugar. Pipe the remaining buttercream in rosettes around the top and decorate with jellied lemon slices.

Makes one 18 cm (7 inch) layer cake (8 slices)

Variations: Coffee – Omit the vanilla and replace the water with coffee essence or very strong black coffee.
Coffee fudge – Make as for coffee but replace the caster sugar with light soft brown sugar.
Orange or lemon – Omit the vanilla essence and add the finely grated rind of 1 orange or lemon and replace the water with the appropriate fruit juice.
Chocolate – Blend 2–3 level tablespoons cocoa powder with 2 tablespoons hot water; cool and use instead of water.

Buttercream

150 g (5 oz) butter, softened
250–300 g (8–10 oz) icing sugar, sifted
a few drops of vanilla essence
1–2 tablespoons milk, top of the milk, evaporated milk or fruit juice

Cream the butter until soft, and then gradually beat in the icing sugar, adding a few drops of vanilla essence and sufficient milk or fruit juice to give the mixture the required consistency.

The buttercream should be fairly thick but easy to spread. If it is too soft, beat in some more icing sugar.

Makes approximately 375 g (12 oz)

Variations: Coffee – Omit the vanilla essence and replace 1 tablespoon milk with coffee essence or very strong black coffee.
Chocolate – Add 25–40 g (1–1½ oz) melted plain chocolate or dissolve 2 tablespoons sifted cocoa powder in a little hot water and, when cool, beat into the icing in place of the milk.
Orange or lemon – Omit the vanilla essence, replace the milk with the appropriate fruit juice and add the finely grated rind of 1 orange or lemon and a few drops of liquid orange or yellow food colouring, if wished.
Mocha – Dissolve 2 teaspoons cocoa powder in 1 tablespoon coffee essence or strong black coffee; add in place of some of the milk or fruit juice.

Glacé Pineapple Cake

250 g (8 oz) butter, softened
250 g (8 oz) caster sugar
4 eggs, beaten
125 g (4 oz) glacé pineapple, finely chopped
125 g (4 oz) glacé cherries, washed, dried and finely chopped
250 g (8 oz) plain flour
1 teaspoon baking powder
25 g (1 oz) shelled walnuts, roughly chopped
50 g (2 oz) ground almonds
Lemon Buttercream:
175 g (6 oz) butter
375 g (12 oz) icing sugar, sifted
grated rind and juice of 2 lemons

Grease a 23 cm (9 inch) round cake tin and line it with some greased greaseproof paper.

Cream the butter and sugar together until pale and fluffy. Add the beaten eggs, a little at a time, beating well between each addition. Toss the glacé pineapple and cherries in 1 tablespoon of the flour and add to the mixture. Sift the remaining flour and baking powder together and fold into the mixture, together with the nuts.

Spoon the mixture into the prepared tin and smooth the surface with a knife. Bake in a preheated oven, 180°C (350°F), Gas Mark 4, for 1½ hours or until the cake springs back when lightly touched. Cover the top of the cake with greaseproof paper if it is browning too quickly.

Leave the cake in the tin for 5 minutes and then turn out to cool on a wire rack. When cold, remove the greaseproof paper.

Make the lemon buttercream. Cream the butter and gradually add the icing sugar, lemon rind and juice, beating well to give a smooth, spreading consistency. Spread the buttercream over the top and sides of the cake and swirl up with a knife to give a 'spiked' appearance.

Makes one 23 cm (9 inch) round cake (12 slices)

far left: Victoria sandwich

Madeira Cake

250 g (8 oz) butter, softened
250 g (8 oz) caster sugar
250 g (8 oz) self-raising flour
125 g (4 oz) plain flour
4 eggs
grated rind of 2 lemons
4 teaspoons lemon juice
piece of candied citron peel (optional)

Line a 20 cm (8 inch) round cake tin with greased greaseproof paper.

In a mixing bowl, cream the butter and sugar together until light and fluffy. Sift the flours together. Beat the eggs into the creamed mixture, following each addition with a spoonful of flour. Fold in the remaining flour, followed by the lemon rind and juice.

Spoon the cake mixture into the prepared tin and lay 2 or 3 thin slices of citron peel on top. Bake in a preheated oven, 160°C (325°F), Gas Mark 3, for 1¼–1½ hours or until the cake is well risen, firm to the touch and golden brown, and a skewer inserted into the centre comes out clean. Cool on a wire rack and cut into slices to serve.

Makes one 20 cm (8 inch) round cake (8 slices)

Easy Apple Cake

250 g (8 oz) cooking apples, peeled, cored and diced
50 g (2 oz) caster sugar
75 g (3 oz) self-raising flour, sifted
½ teaspoon baking powder
¼ teaspoon salt
25 g (1 oz) shelled hazelnuts, chopped
50 g (2 oz) seedless raisins
1 egg, beaten
¼ teaspoon vanilla essence
4 tablespoons cooking oil
ice cream, to serve

Put the apples, sugar, flour, baking powder, salt, nuts and raisins in a bowl. Mix together the beaten egg, vanilla essence and oil and add to the bowl. Stir well until blended.

Spoon the mixture into a lightly buttered 900 ml (1½ pint) ovenproof dish. Spread out evenly.

Bake in a preheated oven, 160°C (325°F), Gas Mark 3, for 1–1¼ hours until the cake is golden brown and shrinking slightly from the sides of the dish. Serve hot with ice cream.

Serves 4–6

Coconut Cherry Cake

375 g (12 oz) self-raising flour
pinch of salt
175 g (6 oz) butter
250 g (8 oz) glacé cherries, quartered
50 g (2 oz) desiccated coconut
175 g (6 oz) caster sugar
2 eggs, lightly beaten
150 ml (¼ pint) milk

Grease a 20 cm (8 inch) round cake tin and line the base with greased greaseproof paper.

Sift together the flour and salt. Rub in the butter with your fingertips until the mixture resembles fine breadcrumbs. Toss the cherries in the coconut and add to the mixture with the sugar. Mix lightly, then add the beaten eggs with most of the milk. Beat well, then add sufficient extra milk to give a soft dropping consistency.

Pour into the prepared tin, level off the top and bake in a preheated oven, 180°C (350°F), Gas Mark 4, for 1½ hours or until well risen and golden brown. Leave in the tin for 5 minutes, then turn out on to a wire rack to cool.

Makes one 20 cm (8 inch) round cake (8 slices)

right: *Madeira cake; easy apple cake; coconut cherry cake*

Orange Kügelhupf

250 g (8 oz) butter, at room temperature
250 g (8 oz) caster sugar
3 eggs
250 g (8 oz) self-raising flour, sifted
grated rind of 1½–2 oranges
50 g (2 oz) chopped mixed peel

Orange Syrup:
50 g (2 oz) icing sugar, sifted
5 tablespoons orange juice

Topping:
finely pared rind of 1 orange
150 ml (¼ pint) water
50 g (2 oz) caster sugar

Orange Glacé Icing:
125 g (4 oz) icing sugar, sifted
about 1 tablespoon orange juice
orange food colouring

Grease a 1.8 litre (3 pint) kügelhupf fancy ring mould or other ring mould with melted butter.

Cream the butter and sugar together until light and fluffy. Beat in the eggs, one at a time, following each one with a spoonful of the flour to prevent curdling. Fold in the remaining flour followed by the orange rind and mixed peel.

Turn the cake mixture into the prepared tin and level the top. Stand the tin on a baking sheet. Bake in a preheated oven, 190°C (375°F), Gas Mark 5, for about 1 hour or until the cake is well risen and firm to the touch. Turn out on to a wire tray to cool.

For the orange syrup, blend the icing sugar and orange juice together and spoon over the cake while it is still warm. When cold, wrap the cake in foil or store in an airtight container for 24 hours.

For the topping, cut the orange rind into julienne strips and place in a saucepan. Add the water and simmer for 5 minutes. Add the sugar, stir until dissolved and then boil until syrupy. Remove the orange rind with a slotted spoon and drain on kitchen paper.

For the glacé icing, put the icing sugar in a bowl and gradually work in the orange juice and a few drops of orange food colouring to give a spreading consistency.

Stand the cake on a plate and spoon and spread the icing over the top, allowing it to run over the edge and down the sides. Just before it sets, sprinkle with the orange rind.

Serves 8

Variation: Lemon rind and juice can be used in place of orange to make a lemon version, but increase the sugar content to 125 g (4 oz) for the syrup.

Marbled Ring Cake

50 g (2 oz) butter, softened
75 g (3 oz) caster sugar
½ teaspoon vanilla essence
1 egg
125 g (4 oz) plain flour
½ teaspoon salt
1 teaspoon baking powder
65 ml (2½ fl oz) milk
75 g (3 oz) black treacle
1 teaspoon mixed spice
walnut halves, to decorate (optional)
Glacé Icing:
175 g (6 oz) icing sugar, sifted
about 1 tablespoon milk

Grease and flour an 18 cm (7 inch) ring mould or square cake tin. Cream the butter with the sugar and vanilla. Beat in the egg. Sift the dry ingredients together and stir into the mixture alternately with the milk. Beat for 1 minute.

Spoon about one-third of the cake mixture into a small bowl and then mix in the black treacle and mixed spice.

Spoon the light and dark batters alternately into the prepared tin. Run a knife through them in a zigzag pattern to give a marbled effect to the finished cake.

Bake in a preheated oven, 180°C (350°F), Gas Mark 4, until the centre is firm to the touch and a skewer comes out clean. Cool for 15 minutes in the tin, then turn out on to a wire rack to cool completely.

Mix the sifted icing sugar with enough milk to give a spreading consistency. Spread quickly and evenly over the top of the cake and leave to dry. Decorate with walnut halves, if liked.

Makes one 18 cm (7 inch) ring or square cake (6 slices)

far left: *orange kügelhupf*
below: *marbled ring cake*

Lemon and Almond Cake

25 g (1 oz) flaked almonds
125 g (4 oz) butter, softened
125 g (4 oz) light soft brown sugar
2 eggs, beaten
grated rind of 1 lemon
125 g (4 oz) wholemeal self-raising flour
Syrup:
75 g (3 oz) caster sugar
3–4 tablespoons fresh lemon juice

Line the base of a 23 cm (9 inch) round sandwich tin with nonstick baking paper. Tip the almonds into the tin and shake them around so they cling to the sides and bottom.

Put the butter and sugar in a bowl and cream until light and fluffy. Beat in the eggs, a little at a time, then beat in the lemon rind.

Fold in the flour in a figure-of-eight motion until smoothly blended, then spoon into the prepared tin and smooth the top. Bake the cake near the centre of a preheated oven, 180°C (350°F), Gas Mark 4, for 20–25 minutes until well risen and firm to the touch.

Meanwhile, prepare the syrup. Put the caster sugar into a small basin and stir in the lemon juice. Leave to stand, stirring occasionally.

Leave the cooked cake in the tin for 1 minute before turning out upside-down on to a wire rack and peeling off the lining paper.

Spoon the lemon syrup evenly over the hot cake, covering the nuts and allowing it to soak in.

Makes one 23 cm (9 inch) round cake (6 slices)

Rosewater Cake

175 g (6 oz) plain flour
1 tablespoon baking powder
125 g (4 oz) butter, softened
50 g (2 oz) caster sugar
2 tablespoons clear honey
2 eggs, lightly beaten
2 tablespoons rosewater
2 tablespoons milk
75 g (3 oz) chopped mixed peel
75 g (3 oz) sultanas
Icing:
200 g (7 oz) icing sugar
2 tablespoons rosewater
1 tablespoon lemon juice (optional)

Grease an 18 cm (7 inch) round cake tin and line with greased greaseproof paper. Sift the flour with the baking powder into a large bowl and set aside.

Whisk the butter, sugar and honey together in a food processor or beat in a large bowl until the mixture is pale and fluffy.

Add the beaten eggs, about 2 tablespoons at a time, beating well between each addition. If the mixture looks as if it might curdle, gently fold in 1 tablespoon flour.

Fold in the sifted flour and baking powder, and then add the rosewater and milk, turning the mixture over several times, before adding the mixed peel and sultanas.

Pour the cake mixture into the prepared tin and then bake in a preheated oven, 180°C (350°F), Gas Mark 4, for 1 hour 5 minutes. Insert a knife into the cake to see if it is cooked – the knife should come out clean. If the mixture is still slightly sticky, replace the cake in the oven for 5 more minutes.

Cool in the tin for 5 minutes and then turn out the cake on to a wire rack. Remove the lining paper and leave to cool completely.

Make the icing. Sift the icing sugar into a bowl, add the rosewater and then beat until smooth. If the mixture is thick but not pourable, add the lemon juice and beat again.

When the cake is cool, put a large plate underneath the wire rack, and pour the icing over the cake, smoothing where necessary with a palette knife dipped in hot water.

Makes one 18 cm (7 inch) round cake (8 slices)

Cumbrian Lemon Cake

The first Englishmen to enjoy oranges and lemons were the Crusaders, who travelled to the Holy Land during the winter months of 1191–2.

125 g (4 oz) butter, at room temperature
50 g (2 oz) lard
150 g (5 oz) caster sugar
2 large eggs
250 g (8 oz) self-raising flour
2 tablespoons lemon juice
finely grated rind of 1 lemon
50 g (2 oz) candied lemon peel, chopped
1 tablespoon milk (optional)
icing sugar, for dusting

Before you make the cake, lightly butter an 18 cm (7 inch) round cake tin with a removable base.

Cream the butter, lard and sugar together until light and fluffy. Add the eggs, one at a time, with about 1 tablespoon of flour for each, and beat in thoroughly. Fold in the rest of the flour with a metal spoon.

Add the lemon juice and grated lemon rind and the chopped candied lemon peel. Mix well – only add the milk if the mixture seems too stiff. It should be of a firm, dropping consistency.

Pour the cake mixture into the prepared tin and bake in the centre of a preheated oven, 180°C (350°F), Gas Mark 4, for about 1 hour. Check that the cake is cooked through by inserting a small skewer, which will come out clean if the cake is ready. If necessary, continue cooking for up to a further 30 minutes, testing at regular intervals.

Leave the cake to cool in the tin for 5 minutes before turning out to cool on a wire tray.

To serve, simply sprinkle the cake with sifted icing sugar.

Makes one 18 cm (7 inch) round cake (8 slices)

far left: *lemon and almond cake*
above: *Cumbrian lemon cake*

Orange Curd Cake

125 g (4 oz) self-raising flour, sifted
1 teaspoon baking powder
125 g (4 oz) caster sugar
125 g (4 oz) margarine
2 eggs
grated rind of 1 orange
Filling and decoration:
3 oranges
25 g (1 oz) caster sugar
175 g (6 oz) curd cheese

Grease and then line the bases of two 18 cm (7 inch) sandwich tins.

Put the flour, baking powder, sugar, margarine, eggs and orange rind in a bowl. Beat well until light and fluffy. Divide the mixture between the 2 prepared cake tins and smooth the tops.

Bake in a preheated oven, 180°C (350°F), Gas Mark 4, for 30 minutes until the cakes are golden brown and firm to the touch. Cool in the tins for 1 minute, then turn them out and cool on a wire tray.

To make the filling, cut away the rind and all the white pith from the oranges and then cut them into segments. Chop the segments from one ½ orange, place in a bowl with the sugar and curd cheese and mix together well.

Sandwich the cakes together with three-quarters of the curd cheese filling, and spread the rest over the top of the cake. Arrange the remaining orange segments in concentric circles on top of the cake.

Makes one 18 cm (7 inch) sandwich cake (8 slices)

Coffee Fudge Cake

150 g (5 oz) butter or margarine, at room temperature
150 g (5 oz) soft brown sugar
3 eggs
150 g (5 oz) self-raising flour, sifted
1 tablespoon coffee essence or very strong black coffee
1 tablespoon black treacle
chopped almonds or toasted hazelnuts, to decorate
Icing:
125 g (4 oz) butter
250 g (8 oz) icing sugar, sifted
1 tablespoon coffee essence or very strong black coffee
1 tablespoon black treacle

Lightly grease and then line the bases of two 20 cm (8 inch) round cake tins and dredge with flour.

Cream together the butter or margarine and sugar until very light and fluffy. Beat in the eggs, one at a time, following each with a spoonful of the flour. Using a metal spoon, fold in the remaining flour alternately with the coffee essence or coffee and black treacle.

Divide the cake mixture between the 2 tins, level the tops and bake in a preheated oven, 190°C (375°F), Gas Mark 5, for about 20 minutes or until well risen and just firm to the touch. Turn out on to a wire tray and leave to cool.

To make the icing, cream the butter until soft, and then gradually beat in the icing sugar, alternating with the coffee and treacle to give a smooth spreading consistency.

Use about one-third of the icing to sandwich the cakes together, and then spread half of the remaining icing over the top of the cake and mark it into patterns with a round-bladed knife.

Put the rest of the icing into a piping bag fitted with a star nozzle and pipe horizontal lines of shells across the top of the cake. Decorate with almonds or toasted hazelnuts.

Makes one 20 cm (8 inch) sandwich cake (8 slices)

Variation: For a coffee cake, simply leave out the black treacle in both the cake mixture and the icing.

Coffee Buttermilk Cake

175 g (6 oz) self-raising flour
150 g (5 oz) caster sugar
5 tablespoons vegetable oil
4 tablespoons buttermilk
1 tablespoon coffee essence or strong black coffee
2 eggs, separated
chocolate crisp wafers or biscuits, to decorate

Buttercream:
75 g (3 oz) butter, preferably unsalted
1 egg yolk
250 g (8 oz) icing sugar, sifted
a few drops of vanilla essence
a little milk

Grease two 18 cm (7 inch) sandwich tins and line the bases with greased greaseproof paper.

Sift the flour into a bowl, add the sugar and mix well. Add the oil, buttermilk, coffee essence or coffee and egg yolks, and beat well until smooth – about 2 minutes with an electric mixer or 3 minutes if mixing by hand. Whisk the egg whites until stiff and fold evenly through the mixture. Pour into the prepared tins and level the tops.

Bake in a preheated oven, 180°C (350°F), Gas Mark 4, for 25–30 minutes or until well risen and firm to the touch. Turn the cake out on to a wire rack and leave until cold.

For the buttercream, melt the butter in a pan. Remove from the heat and gradually beat in the egg yolk and sifted icing sugar with the vanilla essence and sufficient milk to give the buttercream a light spreading consistency.

Use about one-third of the buttercream to sandwich the cakes together and the remainder to spread over the top.

Arrange the chocolate crisp wafers or biscuits in a wheel design over the top of the cake.

Makes one 18 cm (7 inch) round sandwich cake (8 slices)

far left: *orange curd cake; coffee fudge cake*
above: *coffee buttermilk cake*

Chocolate Pound Cake

250 g (8 oz) granulated sugar
65 ml (2½ fl oz) water
65 g (2½ oz) cocoa powder
250 g (8 oz) unsalted butter, softened
250 g (8 oz) caster sugar
5 eggs, separated
250 g (8 oz) plain flour, sifted
¼ teaspoon bicarbonate of soda
pinch of salt
icing sugar, for dusting

Butter a 23 x 12 cm (9 x 5 inch) loaf tin and line with some greased greaseproof paper. Brush the paper with a little melted butter and then dust lightly with flour.

Dissolve the granulated sugar in the water in a heavy saucepan, stirring constantly. Bring to the boil and cook to 110°C (225°F) on a sugar thermometer. Remove the pan from the heat and dip its base in cold water to arrest further cooking. Add the cocoa powder and stir until smooth. Leave to cool.

Cream the butter with the caster sugar until light and fluffy. Add the egg yolks, one at a time, beating well. Stir in the chocolate syrup.

Sift the flour, bicarbonate of soda and salt together into a bowl and then fold into the chocolate mixture. Whisk the egg whites until stiff. Gently fold one-third of the egg whites into the mixture and then gently fold in the rest.

Pour the cake mixture into the prepared loaf tin and bake in a preheated oven, 180°C (350°F), Gas Mark 4, for 1¼ hours or until a skewer inserted into the centre comes out clean.

Remove to a wire rack and leave the cake in the tin for 10 minutes before turning it out to cool completely. When cool, remove the lining paper. Dust with icing sugar before serving.

Makes one 23 x 12 cm (9 x 5 inch) loaf cake (12 slices)

***left:** chocolate pound cake*
***above right:** chocolate fudge cake*

Chocolate Fudge Cake

125 g (4 oz) plain chocolate, broken into pieces
300 ml (½ pint) milk
250 g (8 oz) self-raising flour
½ teaspoon baking powder
125 g (4 oz) butter or margarine
125 g (4 oz) soft brown sugar
2 eggs, separated
To finish:
1 quantity Chocolate Butter Icing (see page 20)
hazelnuts, toasted

Line and grease two 20 cm (8 inch) sandwich tins. Place the chocolate and the milk in a pan and heat gently, stirring, until melted.

Sift the flour and baking powder together. Cream the fat and sugar until light and fluffy, and then beat in the egg yolks, one at a time. Fold in the flour mixture, and then add three-quarters of the chocolate milk and beat until smooth. Stir in the remaining chocolate milk.

Whisk the egg whites until fairly stiff, and then fold 1 tablespoon of the egg whites into the chocolate mixture to lighten it. Carefully fold in the rest of the egg whites in a gentle figure-of-eight motion with a metal spoon.

Turn the cake mixture into the prepared tins and then bake in a preheated moderate oven, 180°C (350°F), Gas Mark 4, for 40 minutes or until the cakes spring back when lightly pressed. Cool on a wire rack.

Use one-third of the icing to sandwich the cakes together. Reheat the remaining icing and then pour over the cake to coat completely. Decorate with the hazelnuts before the icing sets.

Makes one 20 cm (8 inch) cake

Chocolate Almond Cake

125 g (4 oz) butter or margarine
125 g (4 oz) caster sugar
125 g (4 oz) plain chocolate, melted
4 eggs, separated
125 g (4 oz) ground almonds
50 g (2 oz) plain flour, sifted
Chocolate Butter Icing:
175 g (6 oz) plain chocolate, broken into pieces
1 tablespoon water
25 g (1 oz) butter

Line and grease an 18 cm (7 inch) square cake tin. Cream the fat and sugar together until light and fluffy, then beat in the melted chocolate. Beat the egg yolks into the creamed mixture, and then beat in the ground almonds and sifted flour.

Whisk the egg whites until stiff and carefully fold into the cake mixture in a figure-of-eight motion with a metal spoon.

Pour the mixture into the prepared cake tin and bake in a preheated moderate oven, 160°C (325°F), Gas Mark 3, for 50 minutes–1 hour. Leave the cake in the tin for 5 minutes, then turn out and cool on a wire rack.

Beat the icing ingredients in a basin over a pan of hot water. Cool slightly, then spread three-quarters of the icing over the cake and leave to set. Place the remaining icing in a small piping bag fitted with a writing nozzle and pipe attractive lines over the top.

Makes one 18 cm (7 inch) cake

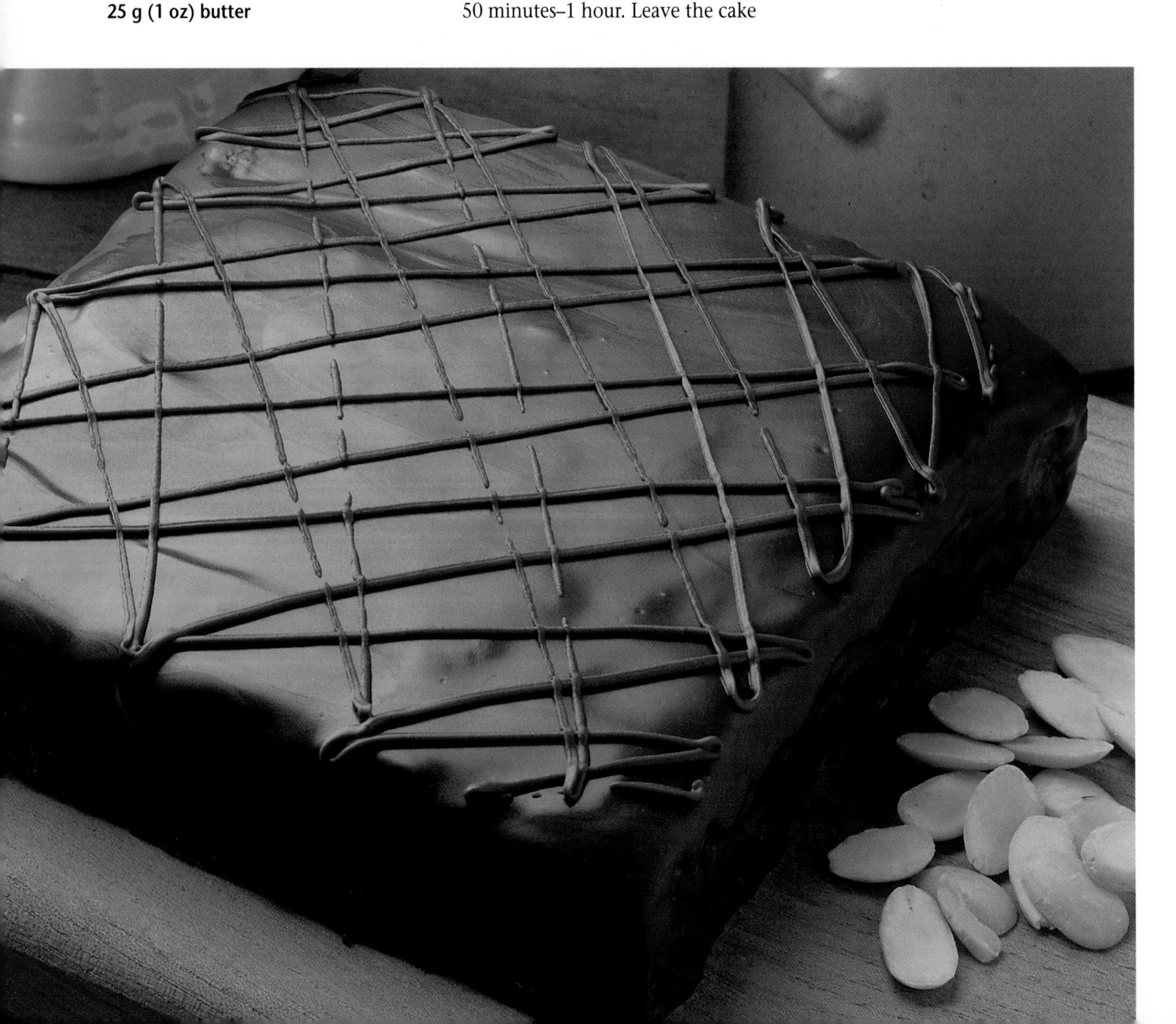

Sachertorte

175 g (6 oz) butter, softened
175 g (6 oz) caster sugar
175 g (6 oz) plain chocolate, melted
8 eggs, separated
125 g (4 oz) plain flour, sifted
Filling and icing:
5 tablespoons apricot jam, warmed and sieved
250 g (8 oz) plain chocolate
2 tablespoons milk
25 g (1 oz) milk chocolate
sugar flowers, to decorate

Grease and flour a 23 cm (9 inch) round cake tin. Place the butter and sugar in a mixing bowl and beat with a wooden spoon for about 10 minutes until pale and fluffy. Alternatively, use an electric whisk. Gradually beat in the melted chocolate until evenly mixed, and then beat in the egg yolks.

Whisk the egg whites stiffly in a separate clean bowl and then fold them carefully into the cake mixture, using a metal spoon. Carefully fold in the sifted flour.

Pour the cake mixture into the prepared tin. Bake in a preheated oven, 160°C (325°F), Gas Mark 3, for 1 hour until firm to the touch. Remove from the oven and cool in the tin for 10 minutes, then turn the cake out on to a wire rack and leave to cool completely.

Split the cake in half and then sandwich together with half of the apricot jam. Brush the top and sides of the cake with the remaining jam.

Melt the plain chocolate in a bowl set over a saucepan of hot water, then remove from the heat and stir in the milk. Pour the chocolate evenly over the cake, using a palette knife to coat the sides. Leave to set.

Melt the milk chocolate in a bowl set over a saucepan of hot water. Spoon into a greaseproof paper piping bag fitted with a thin writing nozzle. Pipe the word 'Sacher' in flowing script over the top of the cake with a flourish beneath.

Decorate with a few sugar flowers, attaching them to the cake with dabs of melted chocolate so that they adhere firmly.

Makes one 23 cm (9 inch) round cake

far left: *chocolate almond cake*
above: *Sachertorte*

Chocolate Potato Layer Cake

The unlikely combination of mashed potato and chocolate makes a light and moist cake, with the rum adding a distinctive richness of flavour.

125 g (4 oz) hot mashed potato
2 tablespoons double cream
65 g (2½ oz) unsalted butter, at room temperature
200 g (7 oz) caster sugar
50 g (2 oz) plain chocolate, melted
¾ teaspoon bicarbonate of soda
2 tablespoons water
3 eggs, separated
125 g (4 oz) plain flour
1 teaspoon baking powder
¼ teaspoon salt
4 tablespoons milk
1½ teaspoons rum
chocolate triangles, to decorate
Rum-cocoa Icing:
40 g (1½ oz) unsalted butter
250 g (8 oz) icing sugar
2 tablespoons cocoa powder
¼ teaspoon salt
1 tablespoon rum
1½ tablespoons strong black coffee

Butter two 18 cm (7 inch) round cake tins and line with greaseproof paper. Brush the paper with melted butter and dust with flour.

Combine the mashed potato with the cream in a heatproof bowl. Keep hot over a pan of hot water. Beat the butter with the sugar until light and fluffy. Add the creamed potato and melted chocolate. Dissolve the bicarbonate of soda in the water and add to the potato mixture. Beat in the egg yolks, one at a time.

Sift the flour, baking powder and salt together twice. Fold them into the mixture, adding alternately with the milk and rum.

Whisk the egg whites until stiff. Gently fold one-third of the beaten egg whites into the cake mixture, and then gently fold in the rest with a metal spoon.

Divide the mixture between the prepared cake tins and bake in a preheated oven, 190°C (375°F), Gas Mark 5, for 30 minutes or until a skewer inserted into the centre comes out clean. Remove from the oven and leave the cakes in the tins on a wire tray for 5 minutes before turning them out on to a wire rack to cool completely.

To make the icing, beat the butter until soft. Sift together the icing sugar, cocoa powder and salt and gradually beat them into the softened butter until well blended. Stir in the rum and coffee.

Sandwich the cakes together with some of the icing and use the rest to cover the top and sides of the cake. Decorate with chocolate triangles.

Makes one 18 cm (7 inch) sandwich cake (8 slices)

right: *chocolate potato layer cake; honey and ginger cake*

Honey and Ginger Cake

250 g (8 oz) plain flour
1 teaspoon ground ginger
125 g (4 oz) butter or margarine
50 g (2 oz) caster sugar
125 g (4 oz) stem ginger, chopped
1 teaspoon bicarbonate of soda
150 ml (¼ pint) milk
50 g (2 oz) clear honey
1 egg, beaten
1 tablespoon demerara sugar (optional)

Line the base of a 15 cm (6 inch) cake tin. Sift the flour and ground ginger into a mixing bowl. Cut the fat into the flour and rub in with the fingertips. Mix in the caster sugar and stem ginger.

Dissolve the bicarbonate of soda in half of the milk and stir in the honey. Make a well in the centre of the dry ingredients and stir in the milk mixture and beaten egg. Mix well, adding more milk as required.

Turn into the prepared tin and level the top. Sprinkle with the demerara sugar, if using. Bake in the centre of a preheated oven, 160°C (325°F), Gas Mark 3, for about 1 hour until set and golden.

Allow to cool and shrink slightly, then remove from the tin and cool completely on a wire tray.

Makes one 15 cm (6 inch) round cake (6 slices)

Chocolate Peppermint Swiss Roll

2 eggs
50 g (2 oz) caster sugar
50 g (2 oz) self-raising flour, less 1 tablespoon
1 tablespoon cocoa powder
extra caster sugar, for dredging

Filling:

50 g (2 oz) butter, at room temperature
75 g (3 oz) icing sugar, sifted
few drops of peppermint essence

Grease and line an 18 x 28 cm (7 x 11 inch) Swiss roll tin.

Whisk the eggs and sugar together until they are light and creamy and the whisk leaves a trail when it is lifted out. (Whisk in a bowl suspended over a pan of hot water if not whisking with an electric beater.) Sift the flour and cocoa together and then gently fold into the mixture with a metal spoon. Turn into the prepared tin and level the top.

Bake the cake in a preheated oven, 200°C (400°F), Gas Mark 6, for 7–10 minutes until it springs back when lightly pressed with the fingertips.

Turn the cake out on to a sheet of greaseproof paper dredged with caster sugar. Trim off the edges and then quickly roll up the cake with the paper inside. Allow to cool.

To make the filling, cream the butter and icing sugar together, and then beat in a few drops of the peppermint essence.

Unroll the cake and remove the greaseproof paper. Spread evenly with the peppermint buttercream, then re-roll. Dredge the cake with caster sugar before serving.

Makes one 18 cm (7 inch) Swiss roll

above: *chocolate peppermint Swiss roll; apricot butterscotch sandwich*
far right: *chocolate Swiss roll*

Apricot Butterscotch Sandwich

175 g (6 oz) butter or margarine, softened
75 g (3 oz) soft light brown sugar
75 g (3 oz) dark soft brown sugar
3 eggs, beaten
175 g (6 oz) self-raising flour, sifted
1 tablespoon black treacle
1 tablespoon lemon juice

Filling:

425 g (14 oz) can apricot halves
150 ml (¼ pint) double or whipping cream
3 tablespoons milk or medium white wine

Grease and line two 20 cm (8 inch) square sandwich cake tins.

Cream the butter or margarine and sugars together until light and fluffy. Beat in the eggs, a little at a time. Fold in the flour with a metal spoon until evenly mixed, then beat in the black treacle and lemon juice.

Divide the mixture between the prepared tins, levelling the tops and making sure that there is sufficient mixture in the corners of the tins.

Bake in a preheated oven, 190°C (375°F), Gas Mark 5, for about 20 minutes or until well risen, golden brown and just firm to the touch. Turn out on to a wire tray and leave to cool. Peel off the paper.

For the filling, drain the apricots and chop half of them. Cut each of the remaining apricot halves into quarters.

Whip the cream and milk or wine together until stiff. Put almost half into a piping bag fitted with a 1 cm (½ inch) plain nozzle. Fold the remaining cream into the chopped apricots.

Use the apricot cream to sandwich the cakes together. Pipe lines of cream over the top of the cake and decorate with pieces of apricot. Serve as soon as possible.

Makes one 20 cm (8 inch) square sandwich cake (8 slices)

Chocolate Swiss Roll

40 g (1½ oz) self-raising flour
15 g (½ oz) cocoa powder
3 eggs
50 g (2 oz) caster sugar
To finish:
caster sugar, for dredging
½ quantity Buttercream (see page 17)

Line and grease a 20 x 30 cm (8 x 12 inch) Swiss roll tin. Sift the flour and cocoa together twice. Whisk the eggs and sugar together in a large bowl until the whisk leaves a trail. Fold in the flour mixture.

Turn the cake mixture into the prepared Swiss roll tin and smooth the surface. Bake in a preheated oven, 200°C (400°F), Gas Mark 6, for 12–14 minutes or until the cake is springy to the touch.

Turn out onto a sheet of lightly sugared greaseproof paper placed on a slightly damp, clean cloth or tea-towel. Remove the lining paper and roll up the Swiss roll tightly from the short edge with the sugared paper still inside. Leave to cool for about 20 minutes.

Unroll the sponge, remove the greaseproof paper and then spread with the buttercream. Re-roll and trim the edges. Chill in the refrigerator until required and serve dredged with more caster sugar.

Makes one 20 cm (8 inch) Swiss roll

Carrot Cake

125 g (4 oz) lime marmalade
2 tablespoons freshly squeezed lime juice
250 g (8 oz) carrots, finely grated
175 g (6 oz) sultanas
125 g (4 oz) unsalted butter, softened
125 g (4 oz) soft light brown sugar
2 eggs
250 g (8 oz) superfine self-raising wholemeal flour
Topping:
125 g (4 oz) low-fat soft cheese
2 teaspoons clear honey
1 tablespoon lime juice
1 tablespoon shredded lime rind, to decorate

Grease and line the base of a 23 cm (9 inch) round springform cake tin. Heat the marmalade and lime juice together in a small saucepan until the marmalade has melted. Remove the pan from the heat and then stir in the carrots and sultanas. Leave to cool while you make the cake.

Put the butter and sugar in a large mixing bowl and beat together with a wooden spoon until light and fluffy. Add the eggs, one at a time, beating well after each addition, until the cake mixture is thick and smooth.

Pour the cooled carrot mixture into the mixing bowl and add the flour, carefully folding it in with a spatula until evenly blended.

Spoon the cake mixture into the prepared tin, level the top and bake in the centre of a preheated oven, 160°C (325°F), Gas Mark 3, for about 1 hour or until the cake springs back when lightly pressed.

Loosen the edge of the cake with a palette knife and release from the tin. Remove the base and lining paper and leave the cake to cool on a wire rack.

To make the topping, beat the soft cheese, honey and lime juice together in a bowl. Spread the topping evenly over the top of the cake and decorate with lime shreds.

Makes one 23 cm (9 inch) cake

Cardamom Cream Cake

125 g (4 oz) butter
250 g (8 oz) caster sugar
2 teaspoons ground cardamom
1 egg, beaten
150 ml (¼ pint) single cream
375 g (12 oz) self-raising flour
thinly pared lemon rind, to decorate
Icing:
about 1 tablespoon lemon juice
125 g (4 oz) icing sugar, sifted

Generously grease a 23 cm (9 inch) ring mould and dust with flour.

Melt the butter and pour over the sugar in a bowl. Beat in the ground cardamom, beaten egg and cream, and then stir in the sifted flour. Turn into the prepared mould and level off the top.

Bake in a preheated oven, 180°C (350°F), Gas Mark 4, for 40–45 minutes or until well risen and pale golden. Leave in the mould for 2 minutes, then cool on a wire rack.

To make the icing, blend the lemon juice into the icing sugar to make a thick flowing consistency. Spoon over the top of the cake, allowing it to run down the sides.

Cut the lemon rind into long thin strips. Put into a basin, cover with boiling water and leave for 5 minutes, then drain and dry well. Use the strips to decorate the top of the cake.

Serves 8

Walnut Layer Cake

This is traditionally a very sweet cake and, if preferred, a smaller quantity of sugar may be used.

250 g (8 oz) butter, at room temperature, or margarine
300–375 g (10–12 oz) caster sugar
250 g (8 oz) plain flour
1 tablespoon baking powder
pinch of salt
250 ml (8 fl oz) milk
4 egg whites
75–125 g (3–4 oz) shelled walnuts, chopped
¼ teaspoon vanilla essence (optional)
8 walnut halves, to decorate

Chocolate Soured Cream Frosting:
75 g (3 oz) plain chocolate, broken into pieces
2 tablespoons water
250 g (8 oz) icing sugar
about 75 ml (3 fl oz) soured cream

Grease and line three 20 cm (8 inch) sandwich tins. Cream the butter or margarine and sugar together until light and fluffy. Sift together the flour, baking powder and salt and mix them into the creamed mixture alternately with the milk, one-third at a time.

Whisk the egg whites until stiff but still moist, and fold into the mixture, alternating with the chopped nuts. Flavour with the vanilla essence, if liked.

Divide the mixture between the prepared tins and then bake in a preheated oven, 180°C (350°F), Gas Mark 4, for about 30 minutes or until springy to the touch.

To make the frosting, put the chocolate in a bowl with the water over a saucepan of simmering water. The hot water must not touch the bottom of the bowl. When soft, stir until smooth and creamy. Sift the icing sugar into a bowl and stir in 2 tablespoons soured cream. Mix in the melted chocolate and add a little more soured cream to give a thick coating consistency.

Spread the cake layers with some of the frosting, sandwich together and swirl the remainder over the top and sides of the cake. Decorate with walnut halves.

Makes one 20 cm (8 inch) three-layer cake (10 slices)

far left: *carrot cake*
left: *cardamom cream cake; walnut layer cake*

Gooseberry Cake

125 g (4 oz) butter
165 g (5½ oz) self-raising flour
1 teaspoon baking powder
2 eggs, beaten
125 g (4 oz) caster sugar
1½ tablespoons white wine
1½ teaspoons orange flower water
½ teaspoon grated nutmeg
125 g (4 oz) gooseberries, topped and tailed
caster sugar, for dredging
cream, to serve (optional)

Grease an 18–19 cm (7–7½ inch) square springform cake tin and line with greased greaseproof paper.

Melt the butter and then cool until only just warm. Sift the flour and baking powder into the butter and mix in the eggs, sugar, wine, orange flower water and nutmeg. Beat together well.

Pour half of the mixture into the tin. Cover with the gooseberries and then add the remaining mixture until the gooseberries are covered.

Bake in a preheated oven, 180°C (350°F), Gas Mark 4, for about 45 minutes or until golden brown and a skewer comes out clean.

Cool in the tin for a few minutes. Dredge with caster sugar and serve hot or cold, with cream, if liked.

Makes one 18–19 cm (7–7½ inch) square cake (6 slices)

Apple Crumb Cake

25 g (1 oz) butter, softened
75 g (3 oz) self-raising flour
25 g (1 oz) caster sugar
1 tablespoon water
1 red dessert apple, cored, sliced and lightly poached, to decorate
Base:
50 g (2 oz) butter, softened
50 g (2 oz) caster sugar
1 egg, beaten
few drops of vanilla essence
125 g (4 oz) self-raising flour
2 cooking apples, peeled, cored and sliced

Grease a 20 cm (8 inch) sandwich tin and line the base with greased greaseproof paper.

For the topping, rub the butter into the flour with your fingertips and stir in the sugar. Sprinkle on the water and mix together until lumpy. Leave on one side.

Make the base. Cream the butter and sugar together until light and fluffy. Beat in the egg and vanilla essence and finally stir in the flour. Spread over the base of the prepared tin. Arrange the cooking apple slices on top and then cover completely with the crumble topping.

Bake the cake in a preheated oven, 180°C (350°F), Gas Mark 4, for about 1 hour until well risen. Cool slightly before turning out the cake onto a wire rack to cool.

Decorate the cake with the poached red apple slices before serving, cut into slices, with whipped cream or crème fraîche.

Makes one 20 cm (8 inch) round cake (6 slices)

far left: *gooseberry cake*
below: *apple crumb cake*

Almond Layer Cake

4 eggs
125 g (4 oz) caster sugar
75 g (3 oz) self-raising flour
50 g (2 oz) ground almonds
few drops of almond essence
50 g (2 oz) toasted flaked almonds
triple quantity icing for Iced Walnut Cake (see page 32)

Grease a 38 x 30 cm (15 x 12 inch) cake tin and then line with greased greaseproof paper.

Beat the eggs and sugar together until thick and the whisk leaves a trail when it is lifted out. Sift the flour and fold into the egg and sugar mixture with the ground almonds and the almond essence.

Spoon the cake mixture into the prepared tin and level off the top. Bake in a preheated oven, 190°C (375°F), Gas Mark 5, for 20 minutes or until the cake is pale golden and springs back when lightly pressed.

Turn out the cake on to a sheet of greaseproof paper and leave to cool. When it is completely cold, cut it across into 3 rectangles.

Spread some of the icing on 2 of the rectangles of cake, sprinkle with some of the flaked almonds and then sandwich the layers together. Spread the remaining icing all over the cake and sprinkle with the remaining almonds. Leave to set in a cool place before serving.

Makes one 30 x 13 cm (12 x 5 inch) sandwich cake (8 slices)

Almond Genoese Sandwich

65 g (2½ oz) plain flour
15 g (½ oz) cornflour
3 eggs
75 g (3 oz) caster sugar
40 g (1½ oz) butter, melted
few drops of almond essence
Decoration:
300 ml (½ pint) double or whipping cream
175 g (6 oz) raspberry or other jam
1–2 kiwi fruit
toasted flaked almonds

Grease and line two 20 cm (8 inch) sandwich cake tins – they may be round or square. Sift the flour and cornflour together twice.

Whisk the eggs and sugar together until very thick and pale and the whisk leaves a trail when it is lifted out. (Whisk them in a basin over a pan of hot water if not whisking with an electric blender.)

Fold in most of the sifted flour, then add the cooled but still liquid butter and almond essence. Finally fold in the remaining flour, quickly and evenly, with a metal spoon.

Pour the cake mixture into the prepared tins and level the tops, making sure that there is plenty of the mixture in the corners of the square tins (if using).

Bake in a preheated oven, 190°C (375°F), Gas Mark 5, for 20–25

minutes until the cakes are well risen and just firm to the touch. Turn out on to a wire rack to cool, then peel off the lining paper.

For the decoration, whip the cream until stiff. Heat the jam a little – just enough to soften it – and then fold it evenly through half of the whipped cream.

Use the raspberry cream to sandwich the cakes together. Spread half of the remaining cream over the top of the cake and mark into swirls. Pipe the remaining cream around the edge, and decorate with the kiwi fruit and almonds.

Makes one 20 cm (8 inch) sandwich cake (8 slices)

Dundee Cake

175 g (6 oz) butter, softened
175 g (6 oz) soft brown sugar
3 eggs, lightly beaten
175 g (6 oz) plain flour
25 g (1 oz) ground almonds
1 teaspoon baking powder
250 g (8 oz) sultanas
250 g (8 oz) currants
75 g (3 oz) chopped mixed peel
75 g (3 oz) glacé cherries, halved
1 teaspoon finely grated lemon rind
1½ tablespoons lemon juice
about 50 split blanched almonds

Well grease an 18 cm (7 inch) round cake tin and line the base and sides with greased greaseproof paper.

Cream the butter and sugar together in a bowl until light and fluffy. Gradually beat in the eggs, adding a tablespoon of the flour with each one. Fold in the ground almonds with a metal spoon.

Sift in the remaining flour and baking powder and fold into the creamed mixture with the dried fruit, mixed peel, glacé cherries, lemon rind and juice.

Spoon the cake mixture into the prepared tin and level off the top. Arrange the blanched almonds on top of the cake and then brush with a little egg white; you can get enough for this by brushing inside the egg shells.

Bake in a preheated oven, 180°C (350°F), Gas Mark 4, for 1 hour, and then reduce the temperature to cool, 150°C (300°F), Gas Mark 2, and bake for a further 1½ hours or until a skewer inserted into the centre of the cake comes out clean.

Leave the cake in the tin for 10 minutes, then carefully turn out on to a wire rack to cool.

Makes one 18 cm (7 inch) round cake (8 slices)

far left: *almond Genoese sandwich*
above: *Dundee cake*

Dark Ginger Cake

175 g (6 oz) black treacle
40 g (1½ oz) demerara sugar
75 g (3 oz) butter
175 g (6 oz) plain flour
2 teaspoons ground ginger
1 teaspoon ground mixed spice
½ teaspoon bicarbonate of soda
2 eggs
125 ml (4 fl oz) milk or buttermilk
a few pieces of stem or crystallized ginger, to decorate

Ginger Buttercream:

2 egg yolks
75 g (3 oz) caster sugar
4 tablespoons water
175 g (6 oz) butter
pinch of ground ginger or mixed spice

Grease a 23 x 12 cm (9 x 5 inch) loaf tin and line with greased greaseproof paper. Put the black treacle, sugar and butter into a pan and heat gently until melted, then cool slightly.

Sift the flour, ginger, mixed spice and bicarbonate of soda into a bowl and make a well in the centre. Add the eggs, milk or buttermilk and the melted treacle mixture and beat until the mixture is smooth.

Pour the cake mixture into the prepared loaf tin and then bake in a preheated oven, 160°C (325°F), Gas Mark 3, for about 1¼ hours or until a skewer inserted into the centre of the cake comes out clean.

Turn out the cake on to a wire rack and leave until cold, then wrap in kitchen foil and store for at least 24 hours before eating.

For the buttercream, beat the egg yolks in a bowl until smooth. Put the sugar and water in a pan and heat gently until the sugar dissolves, then boil steadily until the syrup reaches 110°C (225°F) on a sugar thermometer. Remove from the heat and immediately pour on to the egg yolks, whisking well all the time. Continue to whisk until very light and fluffy.

Cream the butter until soft and gradually beat in the egg and sugar mixture. Flavour with a pinch of ground ginger or mixed spice and spread or pipe over the top of the cake. Decorate the cake with pieces of stem or crystallized ginger.

Makes one 23 x 12 cm (9 x 5 inch) loaf cake (12 slices)

Iced Walnut Cake

175 g (6 oz) butter, softened
175 g (6 oz) light soft brown sugar or caster sugar
3 eggs
175 g (6 oz) self-raising flour, sifted
1 tablespoon black treacle
50 g (2 oz) shelled walnuts, chopped
walnut halves, to decorate

Icing:

150 g (5 oz) caster sugar
1 egg white
1 tablespoon water
1 tablespoon coffee essence or very strong black coffee
a good pinch of cream of tartar

Grease a 20 cm (8 inch) round cake tin and line with some greased greaseproof paper. Cream the butter and sugar together until light and fluffy and pale in colour. Beat in the eggs, one at a time, following each one with a spoonful of flour.

Gently fold in the remaining flour, followed by the black treacle and walnuts. Turn the mixture into the prepared tin and level the top.

Bake in a preheated oven, 180°C (350°F), Gas Mark 4, for 45–50 minutes or until well risen, golden brown and just firm to the touch. Turn out on to a wire rack and leave until cold; then strip off the paper.

Make the icing. Put all the ingredients into a heatproof bowl set over a saucepan of gently simmering water. Stir until the sugar has dissolved, and then whisk well with a hand-held electric mixer or balloon whisk, scraping down the sides of the bowl frequently, until the mixture stands in stiff peaks.

Spread the icing quickly and evenly over the whole cake, using a round-bladed knife to swirl it attractively. Decorate with walnut halves and leave to set.

Makes one 20 cm (8 inch) round cake (8 slices)

above left: *dark ginger cake*
right: *glacé cherry cake*

Glacé Cherry Cake

250 g (8 oz) glacé cherries, halved, washed and dried
125 g (4 oz) self-raising flour
75 g (3 oz) plain flour
25 g (1 oz) cornflour
175 g (6 oz) butter, softened
175 g (6 oz) caster sugar
3 eggs
finely grated rind of 1 lemon
25 g (1 oz) nibbed almonds

Grease an 18 cm (7 inch) round cake tin and line with some greased greaseproof paper. Place the cherries and 25 g (1 oz) of the self-raising flour in a polythene bag, seal and toss to coat the cherries. Sift the remaining flours and cornflour together in a bowl.

Cream the butter and the sugar together until light and fluffy. Beat in the eggs, one at a time. Stir in the sifted flours, lemon rind, almonds and floured cherries.

Spoon the cake mixture into the prepared cake tin and bake in a preheated oven, 180°C (350°F), Gas Mark 4, until well risen and golden. Turn out and cool on a wire rack.

Makes one 18 cm (7 inch) round cake (8 slices)

American Fruit and Nut Cake

175 g (6 oz) stoned ready-to-eat prunes, finely chopped
125 g (4 oz) ready-to-eat dried apricot halves, finely chopped
6 tablespoons dark rum
175 g (6 oz) butter or margarine, at room temperature
175 g (6 oz) dark soft brown sugar
3 eggs
125 g (4 oz) wholewheat flour
125 g (4 oz) plain flour
¾ teaspoon baking powder
¾ teaspoon ground allspice
¼ teaspoon ground ginger
125 g (4 oz) shelled mixed chopped nuts, e.g. almonds, hazelnuts, walnuts, pecans
175 g (6 oz) raisins
grated rind of 1 lemon
grated rind of 1 orange
1 tablespoon black treacle
Topping:
about 4 tablespoons redcurrant jelly, melted
shelled mixed nuts, e.g. Brazils, pecans, almonds, walnuts
a few ready-to-eat prunes
halved glacé cherries

Line the sides of a 20 cm (8 inch) springform cake tin fitted with a tubular base with 2 strips of non-stick silicone or greased greaseproof paper. Put the prunes and apricots in a bowl with the rum. Leave to soak for about 15 minutes.

Cream the fat and sugar together until light and fluffy. Beat in the eggs, one at a time, following each one with 1 tablespoon of the wholewheat flour.

Sift the plain flour with the baking powder and spices and then fold into the cake mixture with the remaining wholewheat flour. Add all the other ingredients, including the soaked prunes and apricots (plus any excess liquid in the bowl), and mix well.

Turn the cake mixture into the prepared tin and level the top. Tie a treble-thickness piece of newspaper around the outside of the tin.

Bake in a preheated oven, 150°C (300°F), Gas Mark 2, for 1¾–2 hours or until a skewer inserted in the centre comes out clean. Leave in the tin until cold, then turn out the cake carefully and peel off the lining paper.

For the topping, brush the cake with the melted redcurrant jelly and then arrange an attractive decoration of nuts, prunes and cherries on the top. Brush again with more jelly and leave to set.

Makes one 20 cm (8 inch) ring cake (14 or more slices)

Crystallized Fruit Cake

This cake is rich and moist. It makes a delightful, light alternative to the traditional iced Christmas cake.

175 g (6 oz) butter, at room temperature
175 g (6 oz) caster sugar
3 eggs, beaten
50 g (2 oz) blanched almonds, chopped
50 g (2 oz) glacé cherries, chopped
25 g (1 oz) crystallized ginger, chopped
25 g (1 oz) crystallized pineapple, chopped
50 g (2 oz) dried ready-to-eat apricots, chopped
50 g (2 oz) ground almonds
175 g (6 oz) plain flour
½ teaspoon baking powder
Topping:
2 tablespoons apricot jam
50 g (2 oz) mixed crystallized chopped fruit

Grease and line an 18 cm (7 inch) round cake tin. Cream the butter and sugar together in a bowl until light and fluffy. Beat in the eggs, a little at a time.

Stir in the chopped almonds, cherries, ginger, pineapple and apricots. Add the ground almonds. Sift the flour and baking powder into the bowl, and then fold into the mixture lightly with a metal spoon until evenly mixed.

Spoon the cake mixture into the prepared tin and smooth over the top. Bake in a preheated oven, 150°C (300°F), Gas Mark 2, for about 2½ hours until the cake is light golden and springs back when pressed with the fingers.

Leave the cake to cool in the tin for 30 minutes, then turn out, remove the lining paper and cool on a wire rack.

Heat the apricot jam in a small pan with 1 tablespoon of water, add the chopped crystallized fruit and spread over the top of the cake.

Makes one 18 cm (7 inch) round cake (8 slices)

far left: *American fruit and nut cake*
below: *crystallized fruit cake*

Lime and Ginger Battenburg

2-egg quantity Victoria Sandwich mixture (see page 8)
grated rind of 1 lime
few drops of green food colouring
15 g (½ oz) stem ginger, chopped
Decoration:
4 tablespoons sieved apricot jam
375 g (12 oz) white marzipan

Grease an 18 cm (7 inch) square cake tin. To line the base, take a rectangular piece of double thickness nonstick baking paper measuring 18 x 25 cm (7 x 10 inches) and make a pleat in the centre. This stands upright to separate the 2 mixtures. Line the sides of the tin with some nonstick baking paper.

Make the Victoria sandwich mixture and then divide between 2 bowls. Add the grated lime rind and a few drops of green colouring to one half of the mixture and stir until evenly blended. Add the stem ginger to the other half.

Place the mixtures separately in each half of the tin, level the tops and bake in a preheated oven, 160°C (325°F), Gas Mark 3, for 40–45 minutes or until the cakes spring back when pressed in the centre. Turn the cakes out, remove the paper and cool on a wire rack.

Trim the edges of the cakes to neaten them. Cut each cake in half lengthways to give 4 strips. Sandwich the strips together with a little warmed, sieved apricot jam, alternating the colours, to make a square. Brush the outside of the cake with the remaining jam.

Blend 1–2 drops of green food colouring into the marzipan. Roll it out and trim to an oblong the same length as the cake, and 4 times its width. Place the cake on the short edge of the marzipan and wrap the marzipan around it, turning the cake over 3 times. Seal the join together underneath the cake.

Knead the marzipan trimmings and roll out three 23 cm (9 inch) pencil-thin lengths of marzipan, plait together and place on top of the cake. Leave to dry.

Makes one 25 cm (10 inch) cake

Fruit Cakes and Teabreads

Banana Honey Teabread

250 g (8 oz) butter, softened
250 g (8 oz) caster sugar
2 tablespoons thick honey
4 eggs, beaten
500 g (1 lb) self-raising flour
½ teaspoon salt
½ teaspoon bicarbonate of soda
4 medium ripe bananas, peeled and mashed
125 g (4 oz) shelled walnuts, coarsely chopped

Lightly grease and line two 23 x 12 cm (9 x 5 inch) loaf tins.

Beat the butter, sugar and honey until light and fluffy. Gradually beat in the eggs, adding a little flour with each addition. Sift the rest of the flour, salt and soda together. Fold into the mixture. Beat in the mashed bananas and nuts.

Spoon into the tins. Bake in a preheated oven, 180°C (350°F), Gas Mark 4, for 1¼ hours until a skewer comes out clean. Cool in the tins, then turn out and remove the lining paper. Wrap in foil, overwrap in polythene bags and store in airtight containers. Serve cut into slices, spread with butter if liked.

Makes two 23 x 12 cm (9 x 5 inch) loaf cakes

Easy No-flour Fruit Cake

500 g (1 lb) mincemeat
500 g (1 lb) mixed dried fruit
125 g (4 oz) glacé cherries, halved
125 g (4 oz) shelled walnuts, chopped
250 g (8 oz) cornflakes, crushed
3 eggs, lightly beaten
1 large can condensed milk, equivalent to 1.2 litres (2 pints) skimmed milk
1 teaspoon ground mixed spice
1 teaspoon baking powder

Grease a 25 cm (10 inch) round cake tin and then line the base with some greased greaseproof paper.

Put all the cake ingredients in a mixing bowl and blend well. Turn the mixture into the prepared cake tin and level the top.

Bake in a preheated oven, 180°C (350°F), Gas Mark 4, for 1¼ hours. Leave the cake in the tin for 10 minutes, and then turn out on to a wire rack to cool.

Makes one 25 cm (10 inch) round cake (12 slices)

right: *prune and nut teabread; easy no-flour fruit cake; banana honey teabread*

Prune and Nut Teabread

250 g (8 oz) wholemeal self-raising flour
pinch of salt
pinch of grated nutmeg
¼ teaspoon ground allspice
1 teaspoon grated orange rind
25 g (1 oz) butter, softened
75 g (3 oz) shelled walnuts, chopped
75 g (3 oz) prunes, stoned and chopped
1 egg
100 ml (3½ fl oz) buttermilk or skimmed milk
3 tablespoons orange juice
soft cheese, to serve

Grease a 15 cm (6 inch) round cake tin. Sift the flour, salt, nutmeg and allspice into a mixing bowl. Tip in any bran remaining in the sieve and stir in the orange rind. Mix in the butter with the walnuts and prunes.

Beat the egg with the buttermilk or milk and orange juice. Pour on to the dry ingredients and mix well.

Turn into the cake tin and bake in a preheated oven, 190°C (375°F), Gas Mark 5, for 40–45 minutes. Leave in the tin to cool, then turn out. Slice and serve with soft cheese.

Makes one 15 cm (6 inch) round cake (8 slices)

Apple, Date and Sesame Loaf

375 g (12 oz) self-raising wholemeal flour
¼ teaspoon salt
¼ teaspoon grated nutmeg
¼ teaspoon ground allspice
¼ teaspoon ground mace
¼ teaspoon ground cardamom
¼ teaspoon ground ginger
1 teaspoon ground cinnamon
grated rind of ½ lemon
50 g (2 oz) Barbados or molasses sugar
2 large eggs, beaten
150 ml (¼ pint) natural yogurt
1 large cooking apple, peeled, cored and grated
250 g (8 oz) stoned dates, chopped
50 g (2 oz) sesame seeds

Grease and lightly flour a 23 x 12 cm (9 x 5 inch) loaf tin. Sift the flour, salt and spices into a large mixing bowl, tipping in any bran left in the sieve. Stir in the lemon rind and sugar and make a well in the centre.

Pour in the beaten eggs and yogurt and gradually mix the dry ingredients into the liquid. Stir in the grated apple with the dates and 25 g (1 oz) of the sesame seeds.

Turn the cake mixture into the prepared tin. Press down the corners and smooth the top with the back of a spoon. Scatter over the rest of the sesame seeds and press them into the top of the loaf.

Bake in the centre of a preheated oven, 160°C (325°F), Gas Mark 3, for 1½–1¾ hours until well risen and lightly browned. Allow the loaf to cool in the tin for 5–10 minutes before turning it out on to a wire rack to cool completely. Store for at least 1 day before serving, cut into slices and buttered.

Makes one 23 x 12 cm (9 x 5 inch) loaf cake (12 slices)

above: *apple, date and sesame loaf*
right: *date and walnut cake*

Date and Walnut Cake

300 ml (½ pint) boiling water
250 g (8 oz) stoned dates, chopped
1 teaspoon bicarbonate of soda
250 g (8 oz) caster sugar
75 g (3 oz) butter, softened
1 egg, beaten
300 g (10 oz) plain flour
1 teaspoon baking powder
½ teaspoon salt
50 g (2 oz) shelled walnuts, chopped
walnut halves, to decorate

Topping:
65 g (2½ oz) brown sugar
25 g (1 oz) butter
2 tablespoons milk

Grease a 23 cm (9 inch) square cake tin and line it with some greased greaseproof paper. Pour the boiling water over the chopped dates and bicarbonate of soda in a bowl and leave to stand for 5 minutes.

In another bowl, cream the sugar and butter together until fluffy, and then stir in the beaten egg with the water and dates. Sift the flour with the baking powder and salt and then fold in to the creamed mixture with the walnuts.

Turn the cake mixture into the prepared tin and smooth the top. Bake in a preheated oven, 180°C (350°F), Gas Mark 4, for 1 hour until cooked. Turn out the cake and leave to cool on a wire rack.

Place all the topping ingredients in a pan and boil for 3 minutes, then spread over the cake. Decorate with walnut halves and leave to set.

Makes one 23 cm (9 inch) square cake (8 slices)

Walnut Streusel Loaf

125 g (4 oz) demerara sugar
25 g (1 oz) butter, melted
125 g (4 oz) shelled walnuts, chopped
1 teaspoon ground cinnamon
Cake:
125 g (4 oz) black treacle
150 ml (¼ pint) milk
2 eggs, beaten
300 g (10 oz) self-raising flour
50 g (2 oz) butter
125 g (4 oz) stoned dates, chopped

Grease a 23 x 12 cm (9 x 5 inch) loaf tin. Mix together the demerara sugar, butter, walnuts and cinnamon for the streusel mixture.

Blend together the black treacle, milk and beaten eggs. Sift the flour into a bowl and rub in the butter with your fingertips until the mixture resembles breadcrumbs. Add the dates and the treacle mixture and mix well together.

Turn half of the cake mixture into the prepared tin and sprinkle with half of the streusel mixture. Cover with the remaining cake mixture and top with the last of the streusel mixture.

Bake in a preheated oven, 180°C (350°F), Gas Mark 4, for 1 hour. Leave in the tin for 5 minutes, then turn out and cool on a wire rack.

Makes one 23 x 12 cm (9 x 5 inch) loaf cake (12 slices)

Peanut and Cranberry Cake

175 g (6 oz) self-raising flour
¾ teaspoon baking powder
125 g (4 oz) wholewheat flour
125 g (4 oz) butter
125 g (4 oz) light soft brown sugar
grated rind of 1 lemon
125 g (4 oz) cranberries, chopped
75 g (3 oz) peanuts, shelled and roughly chopped
50 g (2 oz) chopped mixed peel
2 eggs, beaten with 4 tablespoons milk

Grease a 23 x 12 cm (9 x 5 inch) loaf tin and line with some greased greaseproof paper. Sift the self-raising flour and baking powder into a bowl. Mix in the wholewheat flour. Rub in the butter with your fingertips until the mixture resembles fine breadcrumbs.

Stir in the sugar, lemon rind, cranberries, peanuts and peel. Add the eggs and milk and stir well.

Turn the cake mixture into the prepared tin and level the top. Bake in a preheated oven, 180°C (350°F), Gas Mark 4, for about 1 hour 10 minutes or until cooked.

Turn the cake out on to a wire rack and leave to cool. Wrap in kitchen foil and store in an airtight tin for 24 hours before cutting.

Makes one 23 x 12 cm (9 x 5 inch) loaf cake (12 slices)

Spicy Teabread

500 g (1 lb) self-raising flour
1 teaspoon salt
1 teaspoon ground mixed spice
½ teaspoon ground cinnamon
175 g (6 oz) soft brown sugar
125 g (4 oz) butter
2 eggs, beaten
2 tablespoons black treacle
scant 300 ml (½ pint) milk
½ egg, beaten, to glaze

Grease a 23 x 12 cm (9 x 5 inch) loaf tin. Sift the flour, salt, mixed spice and cinnamon into a mixing bowl. Stir in the sugar.

Rub in the butter with your fingertips. Mix the eggs, treacle and half of the milk together and stir into the flour mixture. Gradually stir in the remaining milk until the mixture drops easily from a spoon.

Spoon the mixture into the prepared tin. Bake in a preheated oven, 190°C (375°F), Gas Mark 5, for 45 minutes–1 hour or until a skewer inserted in the centre comes out clean. Brush with the beaten egg after 30 minutes. Turn out and cool on a wire rack. Cut into slices and spread with butter, if liked, to serve.

Makes one 23 x 12 cm (9 x 5 inch) loaf cake (12 slices)

far left: *walnut streusel loaf; peanut and cranberry cake; spicy teabread*

Apple and Raisin Loaf

250 g (8 oz) grated cooking apple
250 g (8 oz) raisins
150 ml (¼ pint) apple juice
75 g (3 oz) unsalted butter, softened
75 g (3 oz) caster sugar
2 eggs
250 g (8 oz) strong brown flour with malted wheat flakes
2 teaspoons baking powder
1 teaspoon ground cloves
Topping:
1 dessert apple
1 tablespoon lemon juice
4 tablespoons apple juice
2 tablespoons caster sugar
mint sprigs, to decorate (optional)

Grease and line a 1 kg (2 lb) loaf tin. In a bowl, mix together the grated apple, raisins and apple juice.

Place the butter and sugar in a large mixing bowl and beat together with a wooden spoon until light and fluffy. Add the eggs, one at a time, beating well after each addition, and adding 25 g (1 oz) of the flour with the eggs to prevent the cake mixture curdling.

Pour in the apple mixture and the remaining flour, baking powder and cloves. Using a spatula, fold in the apple and flour mixture until evenly blended.

Pour the cake mixture into the prepared tin and then bake in a preheated oven, 160°C (325°F), Gas Mark 3, for 1½–1¾ hours, or until the cake springs back when lightly pressed in the centre. Cool the cake in the tin for 5 minutes, then turn out. Remove the paper and leave the cake to cool on a wire rack.

For the topping, cut the apple into quarters and slice it thinly. Toss the apple slices in the lemon juice to prevent any discolouration. Arrange the slices overlapping on top of the cake.

Heat the apple juice and sugar gently in a small saucepan until the sugar has dissolved. Boil the syrup for 1 minute, then use to brush the top of the cake and the apple slices. Leave to set. Decorate with mint sprigs, if liked.

Makes one 1 kg (2 lb) loaf cake

Apricot and Pine Kernel Cake

175 g (6 oz) dried apricots, finely chopped
grated rind of 1 orange
4 tablespoons freshly squeezed orange juice
50 g (2 oz) pine kernels
125 g (4 oz) unsalted butter, softened
125 g (4 oz) caster sugar
2 eggs
250 g (8 oz) self-raising flour
1 teaspoon ground nutmeg
Topping:
2 tablespoons apricot jam, warmed and sieved
6 dried apricots, halved
1 tablespoon pine kernels
mint sprigs, to decorate (optional)

Grease and line an 18 cm (7 inch) round cake tin. Mix together the apricots, orange rind, orange juice and pine kernels in a small bowl and combine well.

Place the butter and sugar in a large mixing bowl and beat together with a wooden spoon until light and fluffy. Add the eggs, one at a time, beating well after each addition, until the mixture is really thick and smooth.

Sift the flour and nutmeg into the bowl and add the apricot mixture. Using a spatula, fold in the apricot and flour mixtures until evenly blended.

Spoon the cake mixture into the prepared tin, level the top and bake in a preheated oven, 160°C (325°F), Gas Mark 3, for about 1¼ hours or until the cake springs back when lightly pressed in the centre. Cool the cake in the tin for 10 minutes, then turn it out, remove the lining paper and leave the cake to cool completely on a wire rack.

Brush the top of the cake evenly with some of the apricot jam. Arrange the apricot halves and pine kernels on top. Brush with the remaining apricot jam, and decorate with mint sprigs, if desired.

Makes one 18 cm (7 inch) round cake

above left: *apple and raisin loaf; apricot and pine kernel cake*
right: *almond and cherry cake*

Almond and Cherry Cake

175 g (6 oz) unsalted butter, softened
175 g (6 oz) caster sugar
3 eggs
175 g (6 oz) plain flour
1½ teaspoons baking powder
125 g (4 oz) ground almonds
½ teaspoon almond flavouring
175 g (6 oz) glacé cherries, sliced
Decoration:
3 glacé cherries, halved
1 tablespoon flaked almonds
1 tablespoon apricot jam, warmed and sieved

Grease and line an 18 cm (7 inch) round cake tin. Place the butter and sugar in a mixing bowl and beat together with a wooden spoon until light and fluffy. Add the eggs, one at a time, beating well after each addition, until the mixture is thick and smooth.

Sift in the flour and the baking powder and then add the ground almonds, almond flavouring and cherries. Using a spatula, carefully fold in the flour, almonds and cherries until evenly blended.

Spoon the cake mixture into the prepared tin and level the top. Bake in the centre of a preheated oven, 160°C (325°F), Gas Mark 3, for 1¼ hours–1 hour 20 minutes until the cake springs back when lightly pressed in the centre. Leave the cake to cool in the tin.

Turn the cooled cake out of the tin and remove the lining paper. Arrange the halved glacé cherries and flaked almonds on top of the cake and then brush with the apricot glaze. Leave to set.

Makes one 18 cm (7 inch) round cake

Malted Fruit Loaf

500 g (1 lb) dried mixed fruit salad, stoned and finely chopped
125 g (4 oz) demerara sugar
4 tablespoons malt extract
1 tea bag
450 ml (¾ pint) boiling water
1 egg, beaten
375 g (12 oz) strong brown flour with malted wheatflakes
3 teaspoons baking powder
75 g (3 oz) breakfast bran cereal
Topping:
2 tablespoons malt extract

Grease and line a 1 kg (2 lb) loaf tin or use two 500 g (1 lb) loaf tins. Reserve 2 tablespoons of the dried mixed fruit salad for the topping.

Place the remaining fruit salad in a large mixing bowl with the demerara sugar and malt extract.

Add the tea bag to the measured boiling water and leave to infuse for 3 minutes. Remove and discard the tea bag and then pour the tea on to the fruit, sugar and malt extract mixture. Stir well, cover with some clingfilm and leave until cold.

Stir the egg, flour, baking powder and bran cereal into the fruit, using a wooden spoon. Beat for 1 minute until evenly blended.

Pour the cake mixture into the prepared tin, or divide it equally between the 2 smaller tins. Level the top and bake in the centre of a preheated oven, 160°C (325°F), Gas Mark 3, for about 1¼ hours, or 1 hour for the smaller cakes, or until the cake springs back when pressed lightly in the centre. Turn the cake out of the tin, remove the paper and cool on a wire rack.

To make the topping, heat the malt extract in a small saucepan until it bubbles. Brush the top of the loaf with the hot liquid to glaze. Sprinkle the reserved chopped fruit salad in a straight line on top.

Makes either one 1 kg (2 lb) loaf cake or two 500 g (1 lb) loaf cakes

left: *malted fruit loaf*
above: *country fruit cake*
far right: *light fruit cake*

Country Fruit Cake

250 g (8 oz) plain flour
1 teaspoon baking powder
1 teaspoon ground mixed spice
175 g (6 oz) caster sugar
175 g (6 oz) soft margarine
3 eggs
375 g (12 oz) mixed dried fruit
50 g (2 oz) glacé cherries, chopped
1 tablespoon apricot jam, warmed and sieved

Grease and line an 18 cm (7 inch) round cake tin. Sift the flour, baking powder and mixed spice into a large mixing bowl. Add the caster sugar, margarine and eggs and then mix together with a wooden spoon. Beat for 1–2 minutes until the mixture is smooth and glossy.

Add the dried fruit and the glacé cherries and then stir until evenly blended. Spoon the mixture into the prepared tin and level the top. Bake in the centre of a preheated oven, 150°C (300°F), Gas Mark 2, for 2–2¼ hours until a warm skewer inserted in the centre of the cake comes out clean.

Leave the cake to cool in the tin. When the cake is cold, turn it out, remove the paper and brush the top evenly with the apricot jam.

Makes one 18 cm (7 inch) cake

Light Fruit Cake

50 g (2 oz) glacé cherries, coarsely chopped
175 g (6 oz) currants
175 g (6 oz) sultanas
50 g (2 oz) ground almonds
125 g (4 oz) chopped mixed peel
250 g (8 oz) butter, softened
250 g (8 oz) caster or soft light brown sugar
4 eggs, beaten
250 g (8 oz) plain flour
1 teaspoon ground mixed spice
½ teaspoon ground mixed cinnamon
grated rind of 1 orange
2 tablespoons orange juice
2 tablespoons milk

Grease a 20 cm (8 inch) round cake tin and line with some greased greaseproof paper. Mix the dried fruit, almonds and peel in a bowl.

In a separate bowl, cream the butter and sugar together until very light, fluffy and pale. Beat in the eggs, one at a time.

Sift the flour with the spices and then fold into the mixture with the orange rind, followed by the orange juice and milk. Add the dried fruit mixture and fold in.

Spoon the cake mixture into the prepared tin and then bake in a preheated oven, 160°C (325°F), Gas Mark 3, for about 2½ hours or until a skewer inserted in the centre of the cake comes out clean. Leave to cool completely in the tin.

Makes one 20 cm (8 inch) round cake (12 slices)

Earl Grey Fruit Cake

50 g (2 oz) sultanas
50 g (2 oz) raisins
50 g (2 oz) currants
1 teaspoon grated lemon rind
125 g (4 oz) demerara sugar
150 ml (¼ pint) cold strong Earl Grey tea, strained
1 egg, beaten
250 g (8 oz) self-raising flour

Grease a 20 x 10 cm (8 x 4 inch) loaf tin and line with some greased greaseproof paper.

Place the sultanas, raisins and currants in a bowl. Add the lemon rind and all but 1 teaspoon of the demerara sugar. Pour the strained tea over the top, mix well, and then cover and leave to soak overnight.

Add the beaten egg to the dried fruit mixture and combine well. Sift the flour into the mixture and fold in gently with a metal spoon.

Spoon the cake mixture into the prepared tin and sprinkle with the reserved demerara sugar. Bake in a preheated oven, 160°C (325°F), Gas Mark 3, for about 1 hour. Turn out on to a wire rack to cool.

Makes one 20 x 10 cm (8 x 4 inch) loaf cake (8 slices)

Hazelnut and Carrot Cake

250 g (8 oz) carrots
3 eggs, separated
150 g (5 oz) caster sugar
150 g (5 oz) shelled hazelnuts, finely chopped
2 teaspoons finely grated lemon rind
50 g (2 oz) plain flour
½ teaspoon baking powder
icing sugar, for dusting
strips of orange and lemon rind, to decorate

Grease an 18 cm (7 inch) square cake tin. Peel and grate the carrots and re-weigh; you should end up with about 150 g (5 oz).

Whisk the egg yolks and sugar until thick and creamy. Stir in the carrots, hazelnuts and lemon rind. Sift in the flour and baking powder and fold in gently. Whisk the egg whites in a clean, dry bowl until stiff, and then fold into the mixture with a metal spoon.

Turn the cake mixture into the prepared tin and then bake in a preheated oven, 180°C (350°F), Gas Mark 4, for 40–45 minutes.

Leave in the tin for 2–3 minutes and then turn out the cake on to a wire rack to cool. Dredge with icing sugar before serving, and decorate with tied strips of orange and lemon rind.

Makes one 18 cm (7 inch) square cake (8 slices)

Sticky Nut Cake

125 ml (4 fl oz) clear honey
125 ml (4 fl oz) malt extract
125 ml (4 fl oz) milk
125 ml (4 fl oz) sunflower oil
125 g (4 oz) soft light brown sugar
250 g (8 oz) plain flour
125 g (4 oz) mixed whole shelled nuts, chopped
1 egg
1 teaspoon bicarbonate of soda
Topping:
1 tablespoon clear honey
1 tablespoon malt extract
50 g (2 oz) mixed whole nuts, chopped

Grease and line an 18 cm (7 inch) square cake tin. Measure the honey, malt extract, milk, sunflower oil and sugar carefully into a saucepan. Heat gently, stirring occasionally with a wooden spoon, until the sugar has dissolved.

While the honey mixture is warming, sift the flour into a large mixing bowl and add the chopped nuts and egg.

Add the bicarbonate of soda to the mixture in the saucepan and stir until dissolved. Add this to the flour, nuts and egg. Stir well until it is all evenly blended, then beat for 1 minute until smooth and glossy.

Pour the cake mixture into the prepared tin and bake in the centre of a preheated oven, 160°C (325°F), Gas Mark 3, for about 1¼ hours or until the cake springs back when pressed lightly in the centre. Leave to cool in the tin for 10 minutes before turning out the cake. Remove the paper and cool on a wire rack.

To make the topping, heat the honey and malt extract together in a small saucepan. Bring to the boil, remove the pan from the heat and stir in the nuts. Spread the nut mixture over the top of the cake and leave to set.

Makes one 18 cm (7 inch) square cake

far left: *Earl Grey fruit cake; hazelnut and carrot cake*
below: *sticky nut cake*

Snowman Christmas Cake

250 g (8 oz) seedless raisins
250 g (8 oz) currants
250 g (8 oz) sultanas
125 g (4 oz) cut mixed peel
50 g (2 oz) blanched almonds, chopped
50 g (2 oz) glacé cherries, washed, dried and quartered
grated rind of 1 lemon
250 g (8 oz) butter, softened
250 g (8 oz) soft dark brown sugar
4 eggs, beaten
250 g (8 oz) plain flour
1 teaspoon mixed spice
½ teaspoon ground cinnamon
¼ teaspoon ground nutmeg
2 tablespoons brandy

Royal Icing:

whites of 4 large eggs
1 kg (2 lb) icing sugar, sifted
1 teaspoon lemon juice
2 teaspoons glycerine

Decoration:

4 tablespoons apricot jam, warmed and sieved
750 g (1½ lb) marzipan, rolled out
½ quantity moulding or fondant icing
red, green, orange and brown food colourings
extra icing sugar, sifted

Grease and line a 20 cm (8 inch) round deep cake tin. Combine the raisins, currants, sultanas, peel, almonds, cherries and lemon rind.

Beat the butter and sugar with a wooden spoon for 5 minutes until light and fluffy. Beat in the eggs, a little at a time, sifting in a little flour with each addition.

Sift the flour with the spices into the bowl and fold in gently with a metal spoon. Fold in the brandy, then mix in the fruit mixture.

Turn into the prepared tin and smooth the top. Wrap several thicknesses of brown paper or newspaper round the outside of the tin and bake in a preheated oven, 150°C (300°F), Gas Mark 2, for 3½–3¾ hours until a skewer inserted in the centre comes out clean.

Remove the cake from the oven and cool in the tin, then turn out on to a wire rack and remove the lining paper. When cold, wrap the cake in kitchen foil and store in an airtight tin until required.

Brush the top and sides of the cake with apricot jam, cover with marzipan and leave to dry. Attach to a cake board with a little icing.

Make the royal icing. Beat the egg whites in a large bowl until just frothy. Add half of the icing sugar and beat until fluffy and light. Beat in the lemon juice and glycerine and then the remaining icing sugar. This takes about 5–10 minutes so it's best to use an electric whisk. Cover the bowl with a damp cloth and leave to stand for 1–2 hours.

Flat-ice the top of the cake only with half of the royal icing, giving it 2 coats. Leave to dry. Thicken the rest of the icing with extra icing sugar, and then use most of it to rough-ice the sides of the cake, pulling the icing up into peaks with a palette knife.

Colour one-quarter of the moulding or fondant icing green and shape into 14 holly leaves. Reserve the trimmings. Colour a little of the remaining icing red and make some small berries, reserving the remainder. Leave the holly and berries to dry.

Shape some of the uncoloured icing into 2 balls, for the head and body of the snowman. Press them gently together. Make a hat with the remaining red icing, and place on the head. Colour a little of the uncoloured icing orange. Make 3 thin ropes of red, green and orange icing and twist them together to form a scarf, snipping the ends with scissors for tassels. Wrap around the snowman. Make a nose with a small piece of orange icing and three buttons with red icing. Colour a little of the uncoloured icing brown and shape a broomstick and eyes.

Place the snowman with the broomstick on the centre of the cake and make snowballs with the remaining uncoloured icing. Place the snowballs on top of the cake in piles around the snowman and arrange groups of holly leaves and berries around the top of the cake. Dust the snowman with a little icing sugar, for snow. Leave to set completely.

Makes one 20 cm (8 inch) round cake

left: snowman Christmas cake

Fondant-iced Christmas Cake

1 x 20 cm (8 inch) round Christmas cake (see recipe opposite)
Icing and decoration:
550 g (1 lb 2 oz) marzipan, rolled out
23 cm (9 inch) round silver cake board
375 g (12 oz) icing sugar, sifted
1 egg white
1 tablespoon liquid glucose, warmed
icing sugar
egg white, for brushing
red and green food colouring

Bake the cake, wrap in kitchen foil and leave to mature for about 2–3 months. Cover the cake with marzipan 1–2 weeks before icing and place on the silver cake board.

To make the fondant icing, place the icing sugar, egg white and glucose in a bowl and mix, using a palette knife, until a dough is formed. Knead lightly until smooth. Roll out on a surface dusted with icing sugar. Brush the cake with egg white and cover with the icing, reserving any trimmings. Allow to dry overnight.

Colour some of the reserved trimmings green and some red and mould to resemble holly leaves and berries. Arrange in a circle on top of the cake and secure a candle in the centre. Tie a ribbon around the cake.

Makes one 20 cm (8 inch) round cake

Miniature Christmas Cakes

These cakes make wonderful presents for those living alone, or to add to a Christmas hamper.

1 quantity Christmas cake mixture (see recipe, page 48)
Decoration:
4 tablespoons apricot jam, warmed and sieved
750 g (1½ lb) marzipan, rolled out
4 x 18 cm (7 inch) round silver cake boards
royal icing made with 750 g (1½ lb) icing sugar and whites of 3 large eggs (see pages 48–49)
silver dragees
icing Christmas roses
holly leaves and berries (see page 49)
½ quantity moulded or fondant icing (see page 49)
red, yellow and green food colourings
1 metre (1 yard) Christmas ribbon

To make the individual cake cases, cut out four 25 cm (10 inch) circles of double thickness foil and mould each piece around the base and sides of an 875 g (1¾ lb) can to make a 10 cm (4 inch) case. Remove the can carefully and place the cake cases on a baking sheet covered with double-thickness brown paper.

Divide the cake mixture evenly among the foil cases and smooth the tops. Bake the cakes in a preheated oven, 140°C (275°F), Gas Mark 1, for 1¾–2 hours. Remove from the oven and allow to cool slightly, then remove the foil and leave to cool completely.

Brush the tops and sides of the cakes with the jam, then cover with marzipan, reserving the trimmings. Leave to dry, then attach the cakes to the cake boards with some icing.

Cake 1 – flat-ice the top of the cake with some royal icing and then allow to dry a little. Rough-ice the sides of the cake, swirling the icing into peaks with a palette knife.

Make a template to fit the top of the cake. Fold into 8 and cut off a diagonal piece to form a star shape.

Mark the design on the cake, using a pin. Fill a paper piping bag, fitted with a star nozzle, with royal icing. Pipe along the outline of the star. Press a silver dragee into each point of the star. Pipe around the top and base of the cake and then place a Christmas rose in the centre.

Cake 2 – rough-ice all over the cake with royal icing. Decorate with holly leaves and berries.

Cake 3 – cover the cake with some moulding or fondant icing and reserve the trimmings to make the decorations. Using a plain nozzle and the royal icing already in the piping bag, pipe 'Merry Christmas' across the top. Colour a little icing red and over-pipe the letters. Decorate with holly leaves and berries. Tie a ribbon round the cake.

Cake 4 – cover the cake with some moulding or fondant icing and reserve the icing trimmings for decorations. Decorate with holly leaves and berries and a red candle shape with a yellow flame. Tie a ribbon round the cake.

To make the decorations, divide the reserved trimmings into 4 pieces. Keep one white and colour the other three red, green and yellow. Use white for the Christmas rose; red for the candle and holly berries; green for the holly leaves; and yellow for the candle flame.

Makes four 10 cm (4 inch) round cakes

***left:** miniature Christmas cakes*

Simnel Cake

500 g (1 lb) yellow marzipan
375 g (12 oz) mixed dried fruit
50 g (2 oz) blanched almonds, chopped
50 g (2 oz) glacé cherries, chopped
250 g (8 oz) strong brown flour with malted wheatflakes
3 teaspoons mixed spice
175 g (6 oz) soft brown sugar
175 g (6 oz) soft margarine or butter
3 eggs
2 tablespoons apricot jam, warmed and sieved
Decoration:
sugar-coated chocolate eggs
fluffy chick
1 metre (1 yard) 1.5 cm (¾ inch) plain yellow ribbon
1 metre (1 yard) 3 mm (⅛ inch) spotted yellow ribbon

Grease an 18 cm (7 inch) round cake tin and line with some greased greaseproof paper. Roll out 175 g (6 oz) of the marzipan to an 18 cm (7 inch) round using the base of the cake tin as a guide.

Mix together in a bowl the dried fruit, almonds and cherries. Put the flour, mixed spice, brown sugar, margarine or butter and eggs in a large mixing bowl. Mix together with a wooden spoon and then beat for 1–2 minutes until smooth and glossy. Add the fruit mixture and mix well.

Spoon half of the mixture into the prepared tin and level the surface. Place the marzipan round on top. Spoon the remaining cake mixture into the tin and level the top. Bake the cake in the centre of a preheated oven, 150°C (300°F), Gas Mark 2, for about 2½ hours or until the cake springs back when lightly pressed in the centre. Let the cake cool completely in the tin before turning it out and removing the lining paper.

Brush the top of the cake with the warm, sieved apricot jam, then roll out the remaining marzipan to a 20 cm (8 inch) square and cut into 5 mm (¼ inch) strips. Arrange 12 strips in parallel lines a little apart on an 18 cm (7 inch) round thin cake board. Using the remaining strips, weave them one at a time in and out of the strips on the board to make a lattice marzipan square large enough to cover the top of the cake.

Trim the lattice marzipan square into an 18 cm (7 inch) round using the cake board as a guide. Slip the marzipan lattice off the board on to the top of the cake.

Use the leftover marzipan to shape 11 small eggs and a length of thin 'rope'. Press the rope around the edge of the cake and trim to fit. Arrange the marzipan eggs on top.

Place the cake under a hot grill for 3–4 minutes to brown evenly. Leave to cool. When the cake is cold, decorate with the sugar-coated eggs and the chick. Fit the ribbons around the side of the cake and tie in a pretty bow.

Makes one 18 cm (7 inch) round cake

Mother's Day Cake

175 g (6 oz) butter, softened
175 g (6 oz) caster sugar
3 eggs
125 g (4 oz) glacé cherries
50 g (2 oz) crystallized ginger, chopped
50 g (2 oz) crystallized pineapple, chopped
50 g (2 oz) citron peel, chopped
250 g (8 oz) self-raising flour
Icing and decoration:
250 g (8 oz) icing sugar, sifted
2–3 tablespoons water
50 g (2 oz) glacé cherries
2 tablespoons caster sugar
few pieces of angelica

Grease and line a 20 cm (8 inch) round cake tin. Cream the butter and sugar until light and fluffy. Gradually beat in the eggs.

Wash, drain and chop the glacé cherries. Add to the other chopped ingredients and coat them in 2 tablespoons of the flour. Sift the flour over the creamed mixture and fold in gently in a figure-of-eight motion with a metal spoon. Gently fold in the chopped ingredients.

Spoon the cake mixture into the prepared tin. Bake in a preheated oven, 160°C (325°F), Gas Mark 3, for 1¼ hours, then turn out to cool on a wire rack.

Mix the icing sugar with the water and then spoon over the cake, allowing it to drizzle down the

sides. Coat the glacé cherries in some caster sugar and place small pieces of angelica on top of them to form stalks. Arrange the cherries decoratively on top of the cake.

Makes one 20 cm (8 inch) cake

Easter Egg Cake

To make the smaller Easter egg you can use a 2-egg Victoria Sandwich cake mixture and smaller dishes.

3-egg Victoria Sandwich cake mixture (see page 8)
1½ recipe quantities Chocolate Buttercream (see page 9)
red, yellow or green ribbon
selection of marzipan flowers, e.g. daffodils, violets, and marzipan leaves

Divide the cake mixture between two greased and floured oval 600 ml (1 pint) ovenproof glass dishes.

Bake the cakes in a preheated oven, 160°C (325°F), Gas Mark 3, for about 45 minutes or until well risen and firm to the touch. Turn out the cakes on to a wire rack and leave to cool.

Use a little of the buttercream to sandwich the cakes together to give an egg shape. Stand the cake on a cake board.

Use the remaining buttercream to cover the whole cake. Smooth the surface with a palette knife.

Cut a strip of greaseproof paper the same width as the ribbon and lay across the cake, moulding it round as if the cake were tied up, and then place the ribbon over the greaseproof paper. If preferred, you can complete with a ribbon bow on the side.

Arrange a spray of marzipan flowers and leaves on each side of the ribbon, attaching them to the buttercream. Leave to set.

Serves 6

Variations: The cake may be flavoured vanilla, coffee or any other flavour, if preferred, or a Madeira Cake mixture (see page 10) may be used.

above: *Easter egg cake*

Gâteaux

Lemon Cream Sponge

3 eggs
75 g (3 oz) caster sugar
75 g (3 oz) self-raising flour, sifted
150 ml (¼ pint) double cream, whipped
2 tablespoons lemon curd
Decoration:
sifted icing sugar
sugared shreds of lemon rind
twisted lemon slices

Grease two 18 cm (7 inch) sandwich tins and line them with greased greaseproof paper.

Put the eggs and sugar into a heatproof bowl over a pan of hot water and whisk until thick and creamy. Remove from the heat and whisk for a further 2 minutes. Fold in the flour with a metal spoon.

Divide the mixture between the tins and bake in a preheated oven, 190°C (375°F), Gas Mark 5, for 20 minutes or until the tops spring back when lightly pressed. Turn out the cakes on to a wire rack to cool.

Mix the cream with the lemon curd and use to sandwich the cooled cakes. Dredge the top with icing sugar, decorate with lemon shreds and slices and serve.

Serves 6

Orange and Coconut Layer Cake

50 g (2 oz) butter
75 g (3 oz) self-raising flour
3 large eggs
125 g (4 oz) caster sugar
finely grated rind of ½ orange
Filling and decoration:
250–300 g (8–10 oz) full-fat soft cheese
2 tablespoons clear honey
1 tablespoon orange juice
25 g (1 oz) desiccated coconut
grated rind of ½ orange
1 tablespoon caster sugar
50 g (2 oz) desiccated coconut, toasted
2 medium oranges, peeled, sliced and halved

Grease and line a 28 x 18 x 4 cm (11 x 7 x 1½ inch) rectangular tin. Heat the butter gently until just melted, remove from the heat and leave to stand so the sediment sinks to the bottom. Sift the flour twice.

Whisk the eggs and sugar together with the orange rind until thick and pale and the whisk leaves a trail when it is lifted out. Fold in the sifted flour and pour in the butter, without the sediment, and fold in carefully and lightly.

Turn into the prepared tin and bake in a preheated oven, 190°C (375°F), Gas Mark 5, for about 20 minutes or until well risen and firm to the touch. Turn out, cool on a wire tray and remove the paper.

To make the filling, beat the cheese until light and fluffy, then beat in the honey and enough orange juice to give a soft spreading consistency. Stir the coconut, orange rind and sugar into one-third of the cheese mixture.

Cut the cake in half lengthways and sandwich together with the orange cheese filling. Use most of the remaining cheese mixture to cover the whole cake. Coat the sides evenly with the toasted coconut. Arrange the halved orange slices in a line down the centre of the top, and pipe the rest of the cheese mixture down the long edges.

Makes one 28 x 8.5 cm (11 x 3½ inch) sandwich cake (8 slices)

Malakoff Gâteau

1½–2 packets sponge finger biscuits
150 g (5 oz) blanched almonds, roughly chopped
125 g (4 oz) caster sugar
175 g (6 oz) butter, at room temperature
2 egg yolks
6 tablespoons brandy or dark rum
5 tablespoons milk
300 ml (½ pint) whipping cream
toasted flaked almonds, to decorate

Grease and line a 500 g (1 lb) loaf tin. Cover the base with sponge finger biscuits.

Put the almonds and 50 g (2 oz) of the sugar in a small heavy-based saucepan and heat gently until the sugar turns a light caramel colour. Turn on to an oiled baking sheet, leave until cold and then crush this praline finely with a rolling pin or in a food processor.

Cream the butter with the remaining sugar until light and fluffy. Beat in the egg yolks, alternating with 3 tablespoons brandy or rum, and then stir in the crushed praline mixture.

Combine the milk and the remaining brandy or rum and sprinkle 2 tablespoons over the biscuits in the tin, then spread with half of the praline mixture.

Add a second layer of sponge finger biscuits, sprinkle with another 2 tablespoons of milk mixture and cover with remaining praline mixture. Lay a final layer of biscuits on top and sprinkle with the remaining milk mixture. Press down evenly, then cover with a sheet of greased greaseproof or nonstick silicone paper and then with foil. If possible, put a light weight on the cake and chill for at least 12 hours – preferably 24 hours.

Turn the gâteau out carefully on to a serving dish and gently peel off the paper.

Whip the cream and use some of it to cover the whole gâteau. Put the remainder in a piping bag fitted with a star nozzle and pipe diagonal lines across the top of the gâteau. Sprinkle toasted almonds between the rows of cream.

Serves 10

far left: *lemon cream sponge*
above: *orange and coconut layer cake; malakoff gâteau*

Cigarette Russe Gâteau

2 egg whites
100 g (3½ oz) caster sugar
50 g (2 oz) plain flour
50 g (2 oz) unsalted butter, melted
Filling:
250 g (8 oz) full-fat soft cheese
4 tablespoons soured cream
2 teaspoons caster sugar
375 g (12 oz) mixed soft fruit
Decoration:
long chocolate curls
icing sugar, for dusting

Line 3 baking sheets with nonstick baking paper, and then draw three 18 x 10 cm (7 x 4 inch) rectangles on 2 of the sheets of baking paper and turn the paper over.

Whisk the egg whites in a clean, dry bowl until stiff. Gradually add the sugar, whisking well after each addition. Sift in the flour, add the melted butter and then whisk until the mixture is smooth.

Using two-thirds of this mixture, spread within the marked lines of each rectangle. Bake in a preheated oven, 190°C (375°F), Gas Mark 5, for 4–5 minutes until the edges are golden brown. Leave to cool on the baking paper.

Drop 4 teaspoonfuls of the mixture, each spaced well apart, on to the remaining lined baking sheet. Spread out very thinly to make four 10 x 5 cm (4 x 2 inch) rectangles. Bake for 3–4 minutes until golden brown at the edges. Loosen them all and remove from the sheet, one at a time, returning the remainder to the oven meanwhile. Roll the rectangles quickly around an oiled pencil or chopstick to make the curled cigarette russes. Cool on a wire rack. Repeat to use up all the mixture.

To make the filling, beat together the soft cheese, soured cream and sugar in a bowl until smooth. Place in a nylon piping bag fitted with a small star nozzle.

Remove the cigarette russe layers from the paper. Pipe each layer with zigzags of cream filling. Spread soft fruit over 2 layers, reserving some for decoration. Stack the layers together on a serving plate with the cream layer on top.

Arrange the curled cigarette russes and chocolate curls over the top of the gâteau. Decorate with the reserved fruit and then dust with icing sugar.

Makes one 18 x 10 cm (7 x 4 inch) gâteau

above: *cigarette russe gâteau; lime and pomegranate gâteau*
far right: *brandy torte*

Lime and Pomegranate Gâteau

2-egg quantity Whisked Sponge/Genoese mixture (see Lemon Cream Sponge, page 54)
Filling:
4 teaspoons powdered gelatine
3 tablespoons water
250 g (8 oz) full-fat soft cheese
150 ml (¼ pint) natural fromage frais
300 ml (½ pint) ready-made custard
grated rind of 1 lime
1 pomegranate
2 egg whites
Decoration:
150 ml (¼ pint) whipping cream
40 g (1½ oz) macaroons, crushed
mint sprigs

Line 2 baking sheets with some nonstick baking paper and draw a 21 cm (8½ inch) circle on each one. Turn the paper over. Divide the whisked sponge mixture between the marked circles and spread it evenly within the marked lines.

Bake in a preheated oven, 180°C (350°F), Gas Mark 4, for 10–15 minutes or until the cakes spring back when lightly pressed in the centre. Cool the cakes on the paper. Fit 1 sponge round into the base of a 21 cm (8½ inch) springform tin.

Put the gelatine and water in a bowl over a saucepan of hot water, stirring occasionally, until the gelatine has completely dissolved.

Beat together the soft cheese and fromage frais until smooth. Stir in the custard and grated lime rind. Remove the pomegranate seeds and stir half of them into the cheese mixture with the gelatine.

Whisk the egg whites in a clean, dry bowl until stiff and fold gently into the mixture. Pour into the sponge-lined tin and smooth the top level. Place the remaining sponge round on top of the mixture and leave to set for several hours.

Whip the cream until thick and place half in a nylon piping bag fitted with a small star nozzle. Remove the gâteau from the tin. Spread the remaining cream around the sides of the sponge and coat evenly with crushed macaroons.

Pipe a border of cream on top of the gâteau and decorate with mint sprigs. Pipe 2 rings of cream within the border. Fill the spaces between the cream rings with the remaining pomegranate seeds.

Makes one 21 cm (8 ½ inch) round gâteau

Brandy Torte

5 eggs, separated
200 g (7 oz) caster sugar
4 tablespoons grated chocolate
2 teaspoons ground cinnamon
finely grated rind and juice of 1 lemon
100 g (3½ oz) ground almonds
4 tablespoons brandy
125 g (4 oz) dried breadcrumbs
2 teaspoons baking powder, sifted
To finish:
300 ml (½ pint) double cream
grated chocolate
chocolate leaves

Grease a 23 cm (9 inch) loose-bottomed cake tin. Beat the egg yolks and sugar together until light and creamy. Stir in the next 5 ingredients. Whisk the egg whites until stiff, and then fold into the chocolate mixture. Fold in the breadcrumbs and baking powder.

Turn into the cake tin and bake in a preheated oven, 160°C (325°F), Gas Mark 3, for 1–1¼ hours until firm. Cool on a wire rack.

Spread the top and sides of the cake with whipped cream. Press grated chocolate over the sides. Pipe any remaining cream on top and decorate with chocolate leaves.

Makes one 23 cm (9 inch) gâteau

Crush enough brandy snaps to coat the side of the gâteau. Press them on to the side with a broad-bladed knife.

Pipe around the top edge of the sponge with small rosettes of cream and decorate with the reserved pieces of crystallized ginger. Place the cake on a pretty serving plate and refrigerate until required.

Serves 6

Pear and Ginger Gâteau

3 eggs
100 g (3½ oz) caster sugar
75 g (3 oz) plain flour, sifted
400 g (13 oz) can pear quarters, drained
50 g (2 oz) crystallized ginger, a few pieces reserved for decoration, the rest chopped
600 ml (1 pint) double or whipping cream, whipped to form stiff peaks
small cone-shaped brandy snaps

Grease inside a 19 cm (7½ inch) moule à manque or cake tin with butter and then dust the sides with flour. Place a circle of greaseproof paper in the base.

Put the eggs and sugar in a large bowl and whisk over a pan of hot water until the mixture is thick and creamy. Remove from the heat and beat until cool. (No heat is needed if using an electric mixer.) Fold the flour in carefully in 3 batches.

Pour into the prepared tin and bake in a preheated oven, 180°C (350°F), Gas Mark 4, for about 30 minutes, until the sponge is golden brown, springy to the touch and starts to leave the sides of the tin. Turn out the cake on to a wire rack and leave to cool. When the sponge is completely cold, slice it into 2 layers horizontally.

Reserve 8 of the pear quarters and chop the rest. Mix them with the chopped crystallized ginger and 3–4 tablespoons of the cream. Sandwich the sponge layers with the ginger cream mixture.

Coat the outside of the sponge with most of the cream. Pipe cream into the centre of the brandy snap cones, and arrange them alternately with the reserved pear quarters on top of the sponge cake.

Passion Cake

150 g (5 oz) butter
200 g (7 oz) soft light brown sugar
175 g (6 oz) grated carrots
½ teaspoon salt
1 teaspoon ground mixed spice
2 eggs
200 g (7 oz) self-raising flour
2 teaspoons baking powder
125 g (4 oz) shelled walnuts, finely chopped
Icing:
250 g (8 oz) full-fat soft cheese
2–3 tablespoons lemon juice
50 g (2 oz) icing sugar, sifted
25 g (1 oz) shelled walnuts, chopped, to finish

Grease a 20 cm (8 inch) round cake tin and line with some greased greaseproof paper.

Melt the butter and pour into a mixing bowl. Beat in the sugar, carrots, salt, spice and eggs. Sift the flour and baking powder together and add the walnuts. Fold into the carrot mixture lightly with a metal spoon until evenly mixed.

Pour the cake mixture into the prepared tin. Bake in a preheated oven, 180°C (350°F), Gas Mark 4, for 1 hour until firm to the touch and golden brown. Cool in the tin for 5 minutes, then turn out and cool completely on a wire rack.

Beat the cheese until smooth. Gradually beat in the lemon juice, according to taste, and then beat in the icing sugar until well mixed.

Split the cake into 2 layers and sandwich together with one-third of the icing. Spread the remaining icing over the top and sides of the cake, marking with a fork. Sprinkle the top edge with the walnuts.

Serves 8

Variation: Bake in paper cake cases to make small passion cakes. Half-fill the cases, then bake for 20–25 minutes. When cool, spread with the cheese icing and top each with a walnut half.

Spiced Swiss Roll

4 eggs
125 g (4 oz) caster sugar
125 g (4 oz) plain flour
¼ teaspoon ground mixed spice
½ teaspoon ground ginger
caster sugar, for dredging
icing sugar, for dredging
Filling:
125 g (4 oz) butter, softened
250 g (8 oz) icing sugar, sifted
1–2 teaspoons lemon juice
finely grated rind of ½ lemon
175–250 g (6–8 oz) ginger preserve

Grease a 30 x 25 cm (12 x 10 inch) Swiss roll tin and line with greased greaseproof paper.

Put the eggs and sugar into a large heatproof bowl and place over a saucepan of gently simmering water. Whisk until the mixture is thick and pale. (If an electric mixer is used, no heat is required.)

Sift the flour and spices together twice and fold quickly and evenly through the mixture and then turn quickly into the tin, spreading it out evenly to ensure that the corners are well filled.

Bake the sponge in a preheated oven, 190°C (375°F), Gas Mark 5, for 15–20 minutes or until it is a pale golden brown and just firm and springy to the touch.

Turn the sponge out on to a sheet of greaseproof paper or nonstick silicone paper lightly dredged with caster sugar. Peel off the lining paper carefully, trim the edges with a knife and roll up the cake quickly from a short end while still warm with the sugared paper inside. Cool on a wire rack.

For the filling, cream the butter and icing sugar together and add the lemon juice, a few drops at a time, until a spreading consistency is obtained. Stir in the lemon rind.

Unroll the cake carefully and remove the paper. Spread first all over with ginger preserve and then with the filling. Re-roll the cake carefully and dredge with sifted icing sugar before serving.

Serves 6

far left: *pear and ginger gâteau*
left: *passion cake*
above: *spiced Swiss roll*

American Strawberry Shortcake

250 g (8 oz) plain flour
1 tablespoon baking powder
½ teaspoon salt
50 g (2 oz) caster sugar
50 g (2 oz) butter
about 150 ml (¼ pint) milk
375 g (12 oz) ripe strawberries, or 300 g (10 oz) frozen berries
150 ml (¼ pint) whipping cream, whipped with 1 teaspoon caster sugar (optional)

Sift the flour, baking powder and salt together and stir in the sugar. Cut in the butter with a pastry scraper or round-bladed knife.

Stir in just enough milk to make a soft dough. On a lightly floured board, pat – but do not roll – the dough out to a 30 cm (12 inch) wide oblong. Cut out 2 dough rounds of 15 cm (6 inches).

Lay the pastry rounds on a lightly greased baking sheet and bake in a preheated oven, 220°C (425°F), Gas Mark 7, for about 10 minutes until risen and brown.

Reserve 10–12 of the best berries and lightly crush or halve the remainder and spread on one shortcake layer. Spread on some of the whipped cream. Add the second layer and 'frost' with the remaining cream. Decorate the cake with the reserved berries.

Serves 4–6

below: *American strawberry shortcake*
right: *strawberry gâteau*

Strawberry Gâteau

3 eggs
75 g (3 oz) caster sugar
75 g (3 oz) plain flour, sifted
375 g (12 oz) strawberries, washed and hulled
300 ml (½ pint) double cream, whipped until stiff
2 tablespoons Amaretto liqueur
175 g (6 oz) redcurrant jelly
1 tablespoon water
175 g (6 oz) marzipan

Grease three 20 cm (8 inch) sandwich tins and line the bases with greased greaseproof paper. Flour the tins, shaking out any excess flour.

In a bowl suspended over hot water, whisk the eggs and sugar together for about 5 minutes until pale and thick. Remove from the heat and continue whisking for a further 5 minutes. (No heat is needed if using an electric mixer.)

Fold in the flour with a metal spoon, then turn into the prepared tins. Bake in a preheated oven, 200°C (400°F), Gas Mark 6, for 10 minutes until risen and firm to the touch. Turn out the sponges and cool on a wire rack.

Halve sufficient strawberries to completely cover one layer of the sponge. Mash the remaining fruit with a fork.

Put half of the cream into a piping bag fitted with a star nozzle. Fold the crushed strawberries into the remaining cream.

Sprinkle the 2 plain layers of sponge with Amaretto and then sandwich together with half the strawberry cream, and then place a third sponge layer covered with strawberries on top.

Melt the redcurrant jelly with the water. Using a piece of string, measure the circumference and height of the cake. Roll out the marzipan to the exact size. Brush with redcurrant jelly and carefully press on to the sides of the cake. Use the remaining redcurrant jelly to glaze the top of the cake. Chill.

Pipe a decorative border of cream around the edge of the cake before serving, cut into slices.

Serves 8

Croquembouche

This pyramid of choux buns is often served at an Italian wedding. The buns are filled with a delicious liqueur-flavoured cream and then the whole concoction is swathed in spun sugar.

Choux Paste:
150 g (5 oz) plain flour
pinch of salt
300 ml (½ pint) water
125 g (4 oz) butter
4 eggs, beaten
Filling:
450 ml (¾ pint) double cream
3 tablespoons orange liqueur
3 tablespoons icing sugar, sifted
Sugar Syrup:
375 g (12 oz) loaf or granulated sugar
150 ml (¼ pint) water
5 teaspoons liquid glucose

For the choux paste, sift the flour and salt on to a sheet of greaseproof paper. Put the water in a pan with the butter, heat gently until the butter has melted and bring to the boil. When bubbling vigorously, remove from the heat. Tip in the flour, all at once, and beat well until the mixture forms a ball and leaves the sides of the pan clean. Spread the paste out over the bottom of the pan and then leave to cool until the paste is lukewarm.

Gradually beat in the eggs until the mixture is smooth and glossy and has a piping consistency. A hand-held electric mixer is ideal for this task.

Raspberry Ice Cream Cake

3 eggs, separated
4 tablespoons hot water
175 g (6 oz) caster sugar
¼ teaspoon vanilla essence
2 teaspoons finely grated lemon rind
175 g (6 oz) plain flour
50 g (2 oz) cornflour
1 tablespoon baking powder
Filling:
1 litre (1¾ pints) dairy ice cream
250 g (8 oz) fresh raspberries
Decoration:
icing sugar, sifted
fresh raspberries
fresh mint sprigs

Well grease a 23 cm (9 inch) cake tin and line the base with greased greaseproof paper.

Whisk the egg yolks with the water, sugar, vanilla essence and lemon rind until the mixture is thick and creamy. Sift together the flour, cornflour and baking powder. Whisk the egg whites until they stand in stiff peaks. Fold the flours into the egg yolk mixture with a metal spoon, and then the egg whites.

Turn into the prepared tin and bake in a preheated oven, 200°C (400°F), Gas Mark 6, for 25 minutes or until well risen and golden brown. Leave the cake in the tin for 5 minutes, then turn out and cool on a wire rack.

Just before serving, split the cake into 2 layers. Put spoonfuls of ice cream on the bottom layer and top with the raspberries. Replace the top layer of the cake and sprinkle with sifted icing sugar. Decorate with raspberries and mint sprigs. Serve as soon as possible.

Serves 6–8

Put the choux paste into a piping bag fitted with a plain 1.5 cm (¾ inch) nozzle. Pipe the choux mixture into walnut-sized buns on several greased baking sheets, keeping them well apart.

Bake in a preheated oven, 220°C (425°F), Gas Mark 7, for 20–25 minutes or until the choux buns are well risen, golden brown and firm to the touch. Pierce each bun once to allow the steam to escape, return to the oven and bake for a further 2 minutes. Cook on a wire rack.

Whip the cream with the liqueur until stiff and then stir in the sugar. Use to fill the choux buns. A piping bag fitted with a 5 mm (¼ inch) plain nozzle makes filling the buns easier than splitting and filling them – simply insert the nozzle in the steam escape hole.

Put half the quantity of the sugar syrup ingredients into a heavy-based saucepan and then heat gently until dissolved. Bring to the boil and boil rapidly until a temperature of 154°C (312°F) is reached on a sugar thermometer. Remove from the heat immediately.

Arrange a layer of choux buns on a silver board or dish, attaching them with a little sugar syrup. Then gradually build up the pyramid by dipping the base of each choux bun into the syrup so that it will stick to the previous layer of buns. Continue to form a pyramid in this way until the buns are used up.

Heat the remaining sugar syrup ingredients, as before, to the same temperature. Remove the pan from the heat and dip 2 forks into the syrup. Use only a small amount at a time and wind it round and round the pyramid of buns so the sugar pulls into thin threads which stick to the buns. Repeat until all the syrup is used and a faint haze of spun sugar hangs all over the pyramid. If there is not enough spun sugar, then make up another half quantity and repeat the process. Serve as soon as possible.

Serves 20

far left: *raspberry ice cream cake*
below: *croquembouche*

Praline Meringue Layer

The meringue and praline can both be made several days in advance if stored in airtight containers. Simply assemble when required.

4 egg whites
250 g (8 oz) caster sugar
Praline filling and decoration:
75 g (3 oz) caster sugar
75 g (3 oz) unblanched almonds
450 ml (¾ pint) double or whipping cream
ripe strawberries, raspberries, cherries or apricots

Draw a rectangle 30 x 10 cm (12 x 4 inches) on each of 3 sheets of nonstick silicone paper. Place them on 3 baking sheets.

Whisk the egg whites until very stiff. Gradually whisk in the sugar, a spoonful at a time, making sure the meringue is stiff again before adding any further sugar. Put the meringue into a piping bag fitted with a large star nozzle and pipe to completely cover the rectangles drawn on the paper.

Bake in a preheated oven, 110°C (225°F), Gas Mark ¼, for 2½–3 hours, moving the meringues around in the oven after each hour, until dry and crisp and easy to peel off the paper. Leave to cool.

Meanwhile, make the praline for the filling. Put the sugar and the almonds into a small, heavy-based saucepan and heat gently until the sugar melts. Shake the saucepan to coat all the nuts with the sugar syrup, but do not stir. Cook gently until the sugar turns a good caramel colour, shaking the pan gently from time to time.

Put 4 individual almonds on one end of a well-greased sheet, making sure they are evenly coated. Quickly pour the remaining praline mixture on to the other end of the sheet and leave until cold.

Reserving the 4 individual almonds, crush the sheet of praline using a rolling pin or a pestle and mortar, small mouli cheese grater, liquidizer or food processor (but take care as it may well scratch the surface of the bowl).

Assemble the gâteau not more than 45 minutes before required. Whip the cream until stiff; put about one-third of it into a piping bag fitted with a large star nozzle. Fold the crushed praline into the remaining cream.

Place one meringue layer on a plate or board, spread with half of the praline cream and cover with the second meringue layer. Spread over the rest of the praline cream and then top it with the third meringue layer.

Pipe whirls or a zigzag pattern of cream along the top of the gâteau and decorate with the whole caramel almonds and fresh fruit. Chill for 10–15 minutes.

Serves 8

above: *praline meringue layer; Danish apple torte*
far right: *panforte*

Danish Apple Torte

750 g (1½ lb) cooking apples, peeled and cored
grated rind and juice of 1 lemon
50 g (2 oz) granulated sugar
5 tablespoons sweet or medium sherry
28 ginger biscuits
Decoration:
300 ml (½ pint) whipping or double cream
25 g (1 oz) plain chocolate

Slice the apples into a saucepan, then add the lemon rind and lemon juice. Cover and simmer gently for 10–15 minutes until tender.

Remove the lid. Add the sugar and simmer for 10 minutes, stirring occasionally, until a thick purée is formed. Remove from the heat and leave until cold.

Pour the sherry into a small bowl. Dip in one biscuit and place it in the centre of a large flat plate. Dip in 6 more biscuits and arrange them in a circle around the first one, all touching each other.

Spread one-third of the apple purée over the biscuits, keeping within the curved outline. Repeat the biscuit and apple layers, first dipping the biscuits into the sherry, and finishing with a layer of biscuits. Remove any apple purée from the sides of the gâteau and then chill until set.

Whip the cream until stiff and cover the gâteau completely. Melt the chocolate in a heatproof bowl over a pan of hot water. Put into a small paper piping bag. Cut off the tip of the bag and pipe lines of chocolate across the top of the gâteau. Eat on the same day.

Serves 8

Panforte

75 g (3 oz) blanched hazelnuts, toasted and chopped
75 g (3 oz) blanched almonds, toasted and chopped
275 g (9 oz) candied fruit and peel, chopped
2 teaspoons ground cinnamon
large pinch of ground mixed spice
75 g (3 oz) plain flour, sifted
125 g (4 oz) thick honey
100 g (3½ oz) caster sugar
icing sugar, for dredging

Using rice paper, line an 18–20 cm (7–8 inch) plain flan ring standing on a baking sheet. Combine the nuts, candied fruit and peel. Sift in the spices and flour and stir until evenly mixed.

Put the honey and sugar into a saucepan and bring slowly to the boil. Pour on to the nut mixture and stir well until evenly blended.

Spoon into the tin, levelling the top but not pressing down too firmly. Bake in a preheated oven, 150°C (300°F), Gas Mark 2, for 50 minutes or until the cake is almost firm. Cool in the tin and then remove carefully.

Dredge the top of the cake heavily with sifted icing sugar and store wrapped in foil.

Serves 10–12

Banana Roulade

3 eggs, separated
2 teaspoons water
175 g (6 oz) caster sugar
125 g (4 oz) self-raising flour, sifted
125 g (4 oz) walnuts, ground
caster sugar, for sprinkling
Filling:
3 bananas
1 tablespoon lemon juice
300 ml (½ pint) double cream, whipped
icing sugar, to taste
walnut halves, to decorate

Grease and line a 20 x 30 cm (8 x 12 inch) Swiss roll tin. Whisk the egg whites and water together until stiff. Add the sugar, a tablespoon at a time, and continue to whisk until stiff. Lightly beat the egg yolks and fold into the mixture. Fold in the flour and walnuts.

Turn into the prepared tin and bake in a preheated hot oven, 200°C (400°F), Gas Mark 6, for 15 minutes. Turn out on to a sugared sheet of greaseproof paper and remove the lining paper. Roll up with the paper inside and leave to cool.

Mash the bananas with the lemon juice. Fold into half of the whipped cream and add icing sugar to taste. Unroll the sponge and spread with the banana filling. Re-roll and decorate with the remaining cream and walnuts.

Makes one 20 cm (8 inch roll)

Caramel Cream Roulade

5 eggs, separated
125 g (4 oz) caster sugar
50 g (2 oz) ground almonds
½ teaspoon almond essence
300 ml (½ pint) double cream, whipped
Praline:
75 g (3 oz) whole blanched almonds
325 g (11 oz) caster sugar

Grease and line a 20 x 30 cm (8 x 12 inch) Swiss roll tin. Whisk the egg yolks, sugar, ground almonds and almond essence together until pale and thick. Whisk the egg whites in a clean, dry bowl until stiff and then gently fold them into the mixture with a metal spoon in a figure-of-eight motion.

Pour the mixture into the prepared Swiss roll tin and bake in a preheated moderate oven, 180°C (350°F), Gas Mark 4, for 15–20 minutes. Cool, then cover with a

clean damp cloth and leave until the cake is completely cold.

Carefully turn out the cake onto a sugared sheet of greaseproof paper. Peel off the lining paper. Spread the cake with half of the whipped cream and then roll up carefully. Cover the cake with the remaining cream.

Put the almonds and sugar in a small, heavy-based pan and heat gently until the sugar melts. Cook until it turns a rich golden brown. Remove from the heat, pour onto an oiled baking sheet and cool. Crush and then press onto the cake.

Makes one 20 cm (8 inch) roll

Yule Log

4 eggs
125 g (4 oz) caster sugar
90 g (3½ oz) flour
15 g (½ oz) cocoa powder
25 g (1 oz) butter, melted and cooled
caster sugar, for dredging
6 tablespoons double cream
2 tablespoons dark rum (optional)
1 tablespoon icing sugar, sifted

Crème au beurre au chocolat:
75 g (3 oz) caster sugar
4 tablespoons water
2 egg yolks
125–175 g (4–6 oz) unsalted butter, beaten until soft
50 g (2 oz) plain chocolate, broken into pieces
1 tablespoon rum

Decoration:
sifted icing sugar
marzipan holly leaves and berries (optional)

Grease and line a 30 x 25 cm (12 x 10 inch) Swiss roll tin.

Whisk the eggs and caster sugar together until the mixture is very thick and pale and the whisk leaves a heavy trail when it is lifted out. (Place the bowl over a pan of hot water if not whisking with an electric whisk.)

Sift the flour and cocoa powder together twice and fold gently into the mixture with a metal spoon in a figure-of-eight motion, followed by the cooled but liquid butter.

Turn the cake mixture into the prepared tin. Bake in a preheated oven, 190°C (375°F), Gas Mark 5, for 15–20 minutes or until the cake is just firm and springy.

Turn out the cake on to a piece of greaseproof paper dredged with caster sugar. Trim off the edges and quickly roll up the cake, with the paper inside. Allow to cool.

Whip the cream with the rum (if using) until stiff and then stir in the icing sugar. Unroll the cake carefully, remove the paper and spread evenly with the rum cream. Re-roll carefully.

For the crème au beurre, gently dissolve the sugar in a heavy-based pan with the water. Boil steadily for 3–4 minutes or until 110°C (225°F) is reached on a sugar thermometer. Pour the sugar syrup in a thin stream on to the egg yolks, whisking constantly until thick and cold. Gradually beat into the butter.

Place the chocolate with the rum in a bowl over a pan of hot water and stir until smooth and melted. Cool, then beat into the crème au beurre. Coat the cake with the crème au beurre, then mark attractively with a fork. Chill until set. Before serving, dredge the cake lightly with icing sugar and then decorate with some marzipan holly leaves and berries, if liked.

Serves 8

far left: *banana roulade; caramel cream roulade*
above: *yule log*

Chocolate Rum Cake

250 g (8 oz) butter
250 g (8 oz) plain chocolate
125 g (4 oz) caster sugar
3 eggs
125 g (4 oz) maraschino cherries, well drained
125 g (4 oz) shelled mixed nuts (walnuts, toasted almonds and hazelnuts), roughly chopped
2 tablespoons dark rum
250 g (8 oz) plain sweet biscuits, roughly broken

Grease a 23 x 12 cm (9 x 5 inch) loaf tin and line the base with some greaseproof paper. Melt the butter and chocolate together in a small saucepan over a gentle heat. Remove from the heat and cool.

Put the sugar and eggs in a bowl and whisk together until pale and thick. Gently fold in the chocolate mixture, and then add the remaining ingredients. Spoon the mixture into the prepared tin, cover with aluminium foil and freeze.

To serve, unmould the cake on to a serving plate and allow to soften in the refrigerator for about 30 minutes. Cut into slices to serve.

Serves 12–14

Devil's Food Cake

75 g (3 oz) plain chocolate, broken into pieces
175 ml (6 fl oz) strong black coffee
175 g (6 oz) unsalted butter
250 g (8 oz) soft dark brown sugar
50 g (2 oz) vanilla sugar
3 eggs
300 g (10 oz) plain flour
1½ teaspoons bicarbonate of soda
175 ml (6 fl oz) soured cream
Icing:
500 g (1 lb) sugar
300 ml (½ pint) water
2 egg whites, stiffly whisked

Lightly butter three 20 cm (8 inch) sandwich tins and line with some greaseproof paper. Brush the paper with melted butter and then dust with flour.

Place the chocolate in a saucepan with the coffee and stir over a low heat until the chocolate melts. Set aside to cool.

Beat the butter in a mixing bowl until pale and soft. Add the sugars and beat until fluffy. Add the eggs, one at a time, beating well after each addition. Stir in the melted chocolate. Sift the flour and bicarbonate of soda together and fold into the chocolate mixture, alternating, in 2 or 3 additions, with the soured cream.

Divide the mixture between the tins and bake in a preheated oven, 190°C (375°F), Gas Mark 5, for 25 minutes or until a skewer inserted into the centre comes out clean. Remove from the oven and leave in the tins for 5 minutes before turning out the cakes to cool completely on a wire rack.

To make the icing, place the sugar and water in a heavy saucepan and stir over a medium heat until the sugar dissolves. Brush away any sugar crystals that have formed on the sides of the pan with a pastry brush dipped in cold water. Increase the heat and bring to the boil. Cook to the soft-ball stage, 115°C (238°F). Remove from the heat and dip the base of the pan in cold water to arrest further cooking.

Gradually beat the syrup into the whisked egg whites. Continue beating until the icing thickens and loses its sheen. Use immediately to sandwich the cake layers and spread over the top and sides.

Serves 6–8

Chocolate Angel Food Cake

25 g (1 oz) plain flour, sifted
25 g (1 oz) cocoa powder, sifted
140 g (4½ oz) caster sugar
5 egg whites
pinch of salt
½ teaspoon cream of tartar
To finish:
icing sugar
grated plain chocolate
chocolate ice cream or whipped cream, to serve

Lightly flour, but do not butter, an 18 cm (7 inch) springform cake tin, using the base with the central funnel. Sift the flour, cocoa powder and 75 g (3 oz) of the sugar together 3 times and set aside.

Whisk the egg whites with the salt in a mixing bowl until foamy and then add the cream of tartar. Continue whisking until the egg whites form stiff peaks. Add the remaining sugar, beating until the egg whites are firm and glossy.

Sift the flour mixture over the egg whites and gently but thoroughly fold into the egg whites. Pour the mixture immediately into the tin. Bake in a preheated oven, 180°C (350°F), Gas Mark 4, for 30–40 minutes or until a skewer inserted into the centre comes out clean and the cake is springy to the touch.

Remove from the oven and invert the tin on to a wire rack. Leave the cake to cool completely, then run a knife around the sides and unmould from the tin. Dust with icing sugar and sprinkle with grated chocolate. Serve the cake sliced, with ice cream or whipped cream.

Serves 4–6

far left: *chocolate rum cake; devil's food cake*

Belgian Torte

250 g (8 oz) butter, at room temperature
75 g (3 oz) caster sugar
2 tablespoons oil
¼ teaspoon vanilla essence
1 large egg, beaten
500 g (1 lb) plain flour
2 teaspoons baking powder
250 g (8 oz) apricot jam
75 g (3 oz) dried apricots, finely chopped
Topping:
425 g (14 oz) can apricot halves
1 tablespoon sherry
a little icing sugar

Grease a 20 cm (8 inch) cake tin with a removable base, or line the bottom of an ordinary cake tin with some nonstick silicone paper or greased greaseproof paper.

Cream the butter and the sugar together until light and fluffy, then beat in the oil. Add the vanilla essence and beaten egg and beat well. Sift the flour with the baking powder and then gradually work into the creamed mixture. Knead the mixture together as you would for a shortbread dough.

Divide the dough in half and coarsely grate one portion into the tin to cover the bottom evenly. Beat the jam until smooth and spread lightly over the dough layer, taking it almost to the edges. Sprinkle evenly with the dried apricots. Grate the remaining dough evenly over the jam.

Place the tin in a preheated oven, 150°C (300°F), Gas Mark 2, and bake for 1½ hours until lightly browned. Remove from the oven and leave until cool, loosening the torte gently from the sides of the tin with a palette knife as it cools.

For the topping, drain the canned apricots and then boil the syrup with the sherry until it reduces to 3 tablespoons. Cool slightly.

Remove the torte carefully from the tin and slide on to a serving plate. Arrange the apricot halves around the edge of the torte and brush a little syrup over each, allowing it to run down the sides. Sprinkle sifted icing sugar in the centre and serve.

Makes one 20 cm (8 inch) round cake (8 slices)

above: *Belgian torte*
right: *chocolate gâteau*

Chocolate Gâteau

125 g (4 oz) butter, at room temperature
175 g (6 oz) caster sugar
175 g (6 oz) plain chocolate
75 g (3 oz) plain flour
1 teaspoon baking powder
6 eggs, separated
Filling:
250 g (8 oz) plain chocolate
250 ml (8 fl oz) double cream
2 tablespoons brandy
Decoration:
chocolate scrolls
icing sugar

Grease and flour a 20 cm (8 inch) round cake tin with a removable base. Cream the butter and the sugar together until light and fluffy.

Melt the chocolate in a bowl set over a pan of hot water. Add the melted chocolate to the creamed butter, stirring in well.

Sift the flour and baking powder together. Add the egg yolks to the creamed mixture, one by one, incorporating a little flour mixture each time, and beat together well. Stir in the rest of the flour.

Whisk the egg whites in a clean, dry bowl until they stand in soft peaks. Fold the egg whites gently into the chocolate cake mixture.

Pour the cake mixture into the prepared tin and then bake in a preheated oven, 160°C (325°F), Gas Mark 3, for 1 hour until the surface is firm. Leave the cake to cool in the tin for a few minutes before turning it out on to a wire rack to cool completely.

Meanwhile, prepare the filling. Melt the chocolate in a bowl set over a pan of hot water and stir in the cream and brandy. Leave to cool and thicken. When cool, whip the mixture until it becomes lighter in texture and increases in volume.

Slice the cake horizontally into 3 layers and then sandwich each layer with a little of the chocolate cream.

Set the bowl containing the remaining chocolate cream over the pan of hot water to melt it down again, if necessary, and then pour over the cake. Decorate the top with chocolate scrolls and dust lightly with icing sugar.

Makes one 20 cm (8 inch) three-layered cake (8 slices)

Whisking – a vital procedure

Many special occasion gâteaux rely heavily upon carefully whisked mixtures for their success. In whisking, the aim is to introduce and trap air into a mixture that will expand in the heat of the oven and help the cake to rise before it sets. Whisking is a procedure often carried out alongside gentle heating – introducing heat (for instance, by placing a mixture over a pan of simmering water) helps to cook the mixture very slightly enabling the maximum number of air bubbles to be held. The mixture should be whisked until doubled in bulk and until a thick ribbon is left behind when the whisk is lifted out of the bowl.

Whisk mixtures with either a balloon whisk, rotary whisk, electric hand-held whisk or by using the whisk attachment of your food processor if it has one. Electric whisks and food processors certainly cut out much of the wearisome beating and whisking required.

Citrus Mousse Gâteau

1 Genoese Sponge (see page 30 and omit the almond essence)
135 g (4 ¾ oz) packet lemon jelly
150 ml (¼ pint) boiling water
150 ml (¼ pint) lemon yogurt
300 ml (½ pint) double cream
150 ml (¼ pint) cream, whipped, to decorate

Dissolve the jelly in the water. Cool slightly, then whisk in the yogurt. Chill until it begins to thicken.

Whip the cream until it stands in very soft peaks. Whisk into the jelly mixture and leave to set. Use the mixture to sandwich the cake and cover the top. Chill until set. Pipe the whipped cream around the edge to decorate.

Makes one 20 cm (8 inch) gâteau

Chocolate Mallow Gâteau

5 eggs, separated
175 g (6 oz) caster sugar
175 g (6 oz) plain chocolate, melted
2 tablespoons very hot water
To finish:
300 ml (½ pint) double cream, whipped
icing sugar

Grease and line two 20 cm (8 inch) sandwich tins. Beat the egg yolks with the sugar until pale and creamy, then whisk in the melted chocolate and the hot water. Whisk the egg whites in a clean, dry bowl until stiff and then fold them gently into the chocolate mixture.

Turn the cake mixture into the prepared tins and then bake in a preheated moderate oven, 180°C (350°F), Gas Mark 4, for 15–20 minutes until firm to the touch. Leave the cakes in the tins until cool – they will sink a little – and then chill until cold.

Sandwich the cakes together with the whipped cream and dust lightly with icing sugar.

Makes one 20 cm (8 inch) gâteau

left: *citrus mousse gâteau*
below: *chocolate mallow gâteau*
above right: *chocolate swirl gâteau*

Chocolate Swirl Gâteau

250 g (8 oz) medium-fat soft cheese
50 g (2 oz) caster sugar
1 egg
1 teaspoon vanilla essence
Chocolate Mixture:
300 g (10 oz) self-raising flour
25 g (1 oz) cocoa powder
½ teaspoon baking powder
250 g (8 oz) soft light brown sugar
300 ml (½ pint) water
125 ml (4 fl oz) sunflower oil
1½ teaspoons vinegar
Chocolate Cream Icing:
175 g (6 oz) plain chocolate, broken into pieces
300 ml (½ pint) whipping cream
Decoration:
9 white chocolate rose leaves
9 dark chocolate rose leaves

Grease and line two 20 cm (8 inch) round sandwich tins. To make the cheese mixture, place the cheese, sugar, egg and vanilla essence in a bowl. Beat together with a wooden spoon for 1–2 minutes to give a smooth batter.

To make the chocolate mixture, sift the flour, cocoa powder and baking powder into a large bowl. Add the sugar and mix well. Whisk together the water, oil and vinegar and stir into the dry ingredients. Beat with a wooden spoon for 1–2 minutes until glossy.

Divide the mixture evenly between the prepared tins. Drop spoonfuls of cheese mixture into the chocolate mixture and then swirl with a spatula to make streaks.

Bake in the centre of a preheated oven, 180°C (350°F), Gas Mark 4, for 40–45 minutes or until the cakes spring back when lightly pressed in the centre. Turn out the cakes and remove the lining paper. Leave to cool on a wire rack.

To make the chocolate cream icing, put the chocolate and 150 ml (¼ pint) cream in a small saucepan. Heat gently, stirring occasionally, until the chocolate has melted and the mixture is smooth. Remove from the heat and allow to cool.

Whip the remaining cream until thick and fold in 1 tablespoon of chocolate cream icing until evenly blended. Use two-thirds of this cream to sandwich the cakes together. Place the gâteau on a cooling rack with a large plate underneath to catch the drips.

When the chocolate cream icing is thick enough to coat the back of a spoon, pour it over the gâteau to coat it evenly, allowing the excess to fall on to the plate. Spoon any excess icing into the remaining cream and fold in carefully. Place the chocolate cream icing in a nylon piping bag fitted with a small star nozzle.

Transfer the gâteau to a serving plate and pipe around the top and base with chocolate cream icing. Decorate with white and dark chocolate rose leaves.

Makes one 20 cm (8 inch) round gâteau

Small Cakes and Biscuits

Queen Cakes

125 g (4 oz) butter, softened
125 g (4 oz) caster sugar
2 eggs, beaten
125 g (4 oz) self-raising flour
½ teaspoon vanilla essence
50 g (2 oz) sultanas, chopped
1–2 teaspoons milk
To finish:
150 g (5 oz) icing sugar, sifted
2–3 tablespoons warm water
10 glacé cherries, halved

Cream the butter and sugar together until very pale and fluffy. Gradually beat in the eggs, the equivalent of one at a time, adding a little flour between each addition. Stir in the vanilla essence and sultanas, then fold in the remaining flour, adding sufficient milk to make a soft dropping consistency.

Divide the cake mixture equally between 20 paper cases and bake in a preheated oven, 180°C (350°F), Gas Mark 4, for 15 minutes or until the cakes spring back when lightly pressed. Leave the cakes to cool on a wire rack.

To finish, mix the icing sugar with enough water to make a smooth thick icing. Use to ice each cake, and gently press half a glacé cherry on top.

Makes 20

Greek Citrus Diamonds

125 g (4 oz) butter, softened
250 g (8 oz) caster sugar
175 g (6 oz) plain flour
2 teaspoons baking powder
pinch of salt
½ teaspoon ground mixed spice
50 g (2 oz) fine semolina
finely grated rind and juice of 2 oranges
2 eggs
1 tablespoon sesame seeds
Syrup Glaze:
125 g (4 oz) sugar
finely grated rind and juice of 1 orange
2 tablespoons clear honey
Decoration:
2 tablespoons sesame seeds
lightly toasted strips of candied orange peel

Grease a 25 x 18 cm (10 x 7 inch) tin and line with some greased greaseproof paper or nonstick baking paper.

Cream the butter and sugar together until pale and fluffy; this can be done by hand, with an electric mixer or in a food processor.

Sift together the flour, baking powder, salt and mixed spice. Add to the creamed mixture, together with the semolina, orange rind and juice, eggs and sesame seeds. Mix well until blended.

Spread the mixture evenly in the prepared tin and then bake in a preheated oven, 180°C (350°F), Gas Mark 4, for about 1¼ hours until firm but springy to the touch.

Meanwhile, make the syrup glaze. Put the sugar and orange rind and juice into a pan and stir over a gentle heat until the sugar has dissolved. Add the honey and boil gently for 3 minutes.

When the cake is ready, remove it from the oven and pierce it at evenly-spaced intervals with a fine skewer. Spoon the syrup glaze evenly over the top and sprinkle with the toasted sesame seeds. Set aside until completely cold.

Decorate the cake with the strips of candied orange peel. Cut into diamond shapes and serve.

Makes 8–10

Cinnamon Almond Slices

125 g (4 oz) butter, softened
50 g (2 oz) caster sugar
175 g (6 oz) plain flour
½ teaspoon ground cinnamon
a little beaten egg, to glaze
25 g (1 oz) flaked or nibbed almonds
1 tablespoon granulated sugar

Grease a 28 x 18 cm (11 x 7 inch) Swiss roll tin. Cream the butter and sugar together until light and fluffy. Sift in the flour and cinnamon and mix well together.

Press into the prepared tin and flatten with a palette knife. Brush with a little beaten egg and then prick all over with a fork. Sprinkle over the almonds and sugar.

Bake in a preheated oven, 180°C (350°F), Gas Mark 4, for 20 minutes or until golden brown. Cool in the tin and mark into 18 fingers while still warm. When cold, cut into fingers and serve.

Makes 18

far left: *queen cakes*
left: *Greek citrus diamonds; cinnamon almond slices*

Brownies

125 g (4 oz) butter
125 g (4 oz) plain chocolate, broken into pieces
125 g (4 oz) soft brown sugar
125 g (4 oz) self-raising flour
pinch of salt
2 eggs, beaten
50 g (2 oz) shelled walnuts, coarsely chopped
1–2 tablespoons milk

Grease a 20 cm (8 inch) square cake tin. Put the butter and chocolate pieces in a heatproof bowl and warm over a pan of hot water until melted, stirring occasionally. Remove the bowl from the heat. Stir in the sugar and mix thoroughly. Leave to cool.

Sift the flour and salt into a mixing bowl. Make a well in the centre and pour in the cooled chocolate mixture. Mix together. Beat in the eggs and walnuts and then add enough milk to give a soft dropping consistency.

Pour the brownie mixture into the prepared tin and bake in a preheated oven, 180°C (350°F), Gas Mark 4, for about 30 minutes or until a skewer inserted in the centre comes out clean. Leave to cool in the tin before cutting into squares.

Makes about 16

Iced Walnut Squares

3 eggs, separated
125 g (4 oz) caster sugar
125 G (4 oz) shelled walnuts, ground
1 teaspoon plain flour, sifted
To finish:
125 g (4 oz) icing sugar, sifted
2 teaspoons lemon juice
16 walnut halves, to decorate

Grease and flour a 20 cm (8 inch) square tin. Beat the egg yolks with the sugar until thick and light in colour. Stir in the ground walnuts and flour. Whisk the egg whites in a clean, dry bowl until stiff and standing in peaks. Fold gently into the nut mixture with a metal spoon.

Spread out the mixture in the prepared tin. Bake in a preheated oven, 150°C (300°F), Gas Mark 2, for 25–30 minutes until set and lightly coloured. Remove from the tin and cool on a wire rack.

Sift the icing sugar into a bowl and stir in sufficient lemon juice to give a smooth consistency. Spread this over the top of the cake. Cut into squares and decorate each one with a walnut half while the icing is still soft. Allow the icing to set before serving.

Makes 16

Peach and Oat Fingers

125 g (4 oz) butter
125 g (4 oz) caster sugar
125 g (4 oz) self-raising flour
pinch of bicarbonate of soda
125 g (4 oz) rolled oats
1 egg, beaten
2 ripe peaches, skinned and sliced

Grease an 18 cm (7 inch) square cake tin and line with greased greaseproof paper. Melt the butter in a pan. Add the sugar and stir well until the sugar has melted.

Sift in the flour and bicarbonate of soda and then stir in the rolled oats. Cool slightly and then beat in the beaten egg.

Place half of the cake mixture in the prepared tin and arrange the peaches on top, pressing the slices down lightly. Top with the remaining mixture, spreading it gently over the peaches.

Bake in a preheated oven, 190°C (375°F), Gas Mark 5, and cook for 35–40 minutes. Cool slightly in the tin and then cut into fingers. Transfer to a wire rack to cool.

Makes about 14

left: *brownies; iced walnut squares; peach and oat fingers*

Yogurt and Honey Cakes

4 eggs, separated
250 g (8 oz) caster sugar
125 g (4 oz) butter, melted
200 ml (7 fl oz) natural yogurt
¼ teaspoon bicarbonate of soda
300 g (10 oz) plain flour
1 tablespoon baking powder
125 g (4 oz) clear honey
4 tablespoons water
strip of lemon rind
1 cinnamon stick
50 g (2 oz) flaked almonds, toasted

Grease a 33 x 23 cm (13 x 9 inch) shallow tin. Put the egg yolks and sugar in a bowl and whisk by hand over a pan of simmering water, or using an electric whisk on high speed, until light and thick. This takes about 5 minutes.

Whisk in the melted butter. Mix together the yogurt and bicarbonate of soda and stir into the mixture.

In a clean, dry bowl, whisk the egg whites until stiff. Fold them lightly into the mixture with a metal spoon. Sift the flour and baking powder into the mixture and fold in lightly until well mixed.

Pour the mixture into the prepared tin and smooth the top. Bake in a preheated oven, 190°C (375°F), Gas Mark 5, for 25 minutes until the cake is golden brown and springs back when pressed with the fingers. Leave to cool in the tin.

Put the honey, water, lemon rind and cinnamon stick in a saucepan. Heat gently for 5 minutes. Remove the lemon rind and cinnamon stick and pour the syrup evenly over the cake. Sprinkle with the almonds.

Leave until the syrup is cold, then cut the cake into 3 lengthways and 8 portions across.

Makes 24

above: *yogurt and honey cakes; munchy date layer fingers*
far right: *Norwegian apple cakes*

Munchy Date Layer Fingers

Filling:
250 g (8 oz) dates, stoned and chopped
2 tablespoons water
1 tablespoon lemon juice
1 tablespoon honey
pinch of ground cinnamon
Oat mixture:
125 g (4 oz) wholemeal flour
175 g (6 oz) rolled oats
250 g (8 oz) butter, softened

Well grease an 18 cm (7 inch) shallow square cake tin. Put the dates and water in a pan and simmer gently until the dates are soft. Allow to cool, then stir in the lemon juice, honey and cinnamon.

Mix the flour and oats in a mixing bowl and rub in the butter with your fingertips. Press half of the oat mixture into the bottom of the prepared tin. Spread with the date mixture and cover with the remaining oat mixture.

Bake in a preheated oven, 180°C (350°F), Gas Mark 4, for 20–25 minutes. Cool in the tin and then cut into fingers while still warm. Remove the fingers from the tin carefully when quite cold.

Makes 14

Norwegian Apple Cakes

2 eggs
275 g (9 oz) caster sugar
125 g (4 oz) butter
150 ml (¼ pint) top of the milk or creamy milk
175 g (6 oz) plain flour
1 tablespoon baking powder
3–4 Bramley cooking apples

Grease and then flour a 20 x 30 cm (8 x 12 inch) roasting tin. Whisk the eggs and 250 g (8 oz) of the sugar until the mixture is thick and creamy and the whisk leaves a trail when it is lifted out. (Place the bowl over a pan of hot water if not whisking with an electric beater.)

Put the butter and milk into a pan. Bring to the boil and stir, still boiling, into the eggs and sugar. Sift in the flour and baking powder and fold carefully into the mixture so that there are no lumps of flour. Pour the cake mixture into the prepared roasting tin.

Peel, core and slice the apples, and arrange them over the top of the cake mixture. Sprinkle with the remaining sugar.

Bake in a preheated oven, 200°C (400°F), Gas Mark 6, for about 20–25 minutes until well risen and golden brown. Cool in the tin, then cut into slices and serve.

Makes 12

Strawberry Palmiers

250 g (8 oz) fresh or frozen and thawed puff pastry
75 g (3 oz) granulated sugar
300 ml (½ pint) double cream, whipped
75 g (3 oz) strawberries, halved
icing sugar, for dredging

Place the puff pastry on a clean surface sprinkled with half of the sugar. Roll out to a rectangle, about 30 x 25 cm (12 x 10 inches).

Sprinkle with the remaining sugar and press this in with a rolling pin. Take the shorter edge of the pastry and roll it up to the centre. Roll the other side to meet it in the centre. Moisten with water and press together to join the rolls. Cut into 1 cm (½ inch) slices and place well apart, cut-side down, on a dampened baking sheet, flattening them slightly.

Bake the palmiers in a preheated hot oven, 220°C (425°F), Gas Mark 7, for 12–15 minutes, turning them over when they begin to brown, so that both sides caramelize. Transfer to a wire rack to cool.

Spoon the whipped cream into a piping bag which has been fitted with a 1 cm (½ inch) fluted nozzle, and pipe swirls of cream onto half of the palmiers. Arrange a few strawberries on the cream and top with the remaining palmiers. Press down and dredge with icing sugar.

Makes 10

below: *strawberry palmiers*
far right: *chocolate toffee bars*

Chocolate Toffee Bars

175 g (6 oz) butter, softened
75 g (3 oz) caster sugar
275 g (9 oz) plain flour
Topping:
125 g (4 oz) butter
50 g (2 oz) caster sugar
2 tablespoons golden syrup
200 g (7 oz) can condensed milk
125 g (4 oz) plain or milk chocolate

Put the butter and sugar in a bowl and beat until light and fluffy. Add the flour and mix to a soft dough.

Knead the dough lightly on a floured surface, and then roll out and line the base of an 18 x 28 cm (7 x 11 inch) shallow tin.

Bake in a preheated oven, 160°C (325°F), Gas Mark 3, for 35 minutes until just beginning to colour. Leave to cool in the tin.

Make the topping. Put the butter, sugar, syrup and condensed milk in a saucepan. Heat gently until the sugar dissolves. Boil for 5 minutes, stirring until toffee-coloured and thickened. Cool and spread over the biscuit base. Leave until cold.

Break up the chocolate and place in a bowl over a saucepan of hot water until it has melted. Spread the chocolate evenly over the toffee, making wavy lines with a round-ended knife. Leave to set, then cut into 3 lengthways and 8 across.

Makes 24

Nutty Meringues

2 large egg whites
150 g (5 oz) icing sugar, sifted
50 g (2 oz) shelled hazelnuts or almonds, toasted and finely chopped
To serve:
whipped cream and soft fruit or melted chocolate

Put the egg whites and sugar into a heatproof bowl over a saucepan of gently simmering water and whisk until the mixture thickens and stands in stiff peaks. Remove from the heat and beat in the hazelnuts or almonds.

Spoon the mixture into rounds, about 5–6 cm (2–2½ inches) in diameter, onto some baking sheets lined with nonstick baking paper or rice paper.

Bake in a preheated oven, 150°C (300°F), Gas Mark 2, for about 30 minutes or until pale cream in colour and easily removed from the sheets. Leave to cool, then store in an airtight container.

Serve plain or topped with a swirl of whipped cream and a piece of soft fruit or a whole hazelnut. Alternatively, drizzle with melted chocolate.

Makes 10

***right:** nutty meringues; cream horns*

Cream Horns

250 g (8 oz) plain flour
pinch of salt
75 g (3 oz) butter or margarine, diced
150 ml (¼ pint) iced water
75 g (3 oz) lard
lightly whisked egg white, or water
1 tablespoon caster sugar
2 tablespoons raspberry jam
250 ml (8 fl oz) double or whipping cream, whipped

Sift the flour and salt into a bowl. Add half of the butter or margarine and rub into the flour with your fingertips until the mixture resembles fine crumbs. Add the water and work in lightly using a knife. A little more water can be added if necessary to bind the dough together to a soft but not sticky consistency.

Shape the dough into a rectangle on a lightly floured surface, then roll out into an oblong, about 40 cm (16 inches) long. Ease any rounded corners into shape. Mark lightly into thirds.

Using a round-ended knife, dab half of the lard in rough heaps on the top two-thirds of the pastry, leaving a border around the edge. Fold the lower third up over the centre section, then fold the top third down over this, keeping the corners square. Seal the edges with the rolling pin and give the pastry a half turn so that the fold is at the right-hand side.

Roll out the pastry as before and repeat the process, first using the rest of the butter and then using the remaining lard. Roll and fold once more without the addition of any more fat.

Wrap and chill in the refrigerator for 20 minutes or longer before using. As the pastry needs to be cool all the time it is being made, it can be chilled between rollings during hot weather.

Roll out the pastry quite thinly to a 45 x 30 cm (18 x 12 inch) rectangle. Trim the edges and cut lengthways into 10 strips. Cut a small piece diagonally from one end of each strip to make a point. Brush the strips with water.

Place the point of a cream horn tin against the point of a pastry strip. Wind the strip around the cream horn tin so that it overlaps about 1 cm (½ inch) at each turn. Place on a dampened baking sheet. When all the horns have been shaped, put in the refrigerator for 20 minutes to rest.

Brush the pastry horns with some lightly whisked egg white or water and sprinkle with the sugar. Bake in a preheated oven, 220°C (425°F), Gas Mark 7, for 15–20 minutes until golden brown. Remove the horns from the tins with a slight twisting action. Cool on a wire tray.

Heat the jam until it has melted and, with a teaspoon, pour a little into the point of each horn. When the pastry and the jam are both completely cold, spoon the cream into a piping bag, fitted with a large rosette nozzle, and fill each horn with a large swirl of cream. Keep cool until ready to serve. When the horns are filled, eat the same day.

Makes 10

Basic Scones

250 g (8 oz) plain flour
1 teaspoon cream of tartar
½ teaspoon bicarbonate of soda
pinch of salt
50 g (2 oz) butter or margarine
25 g (1 oz) caster sugar
about 6 tablespoons milk
milk, to glaze

Sift the flour, cream of tartar, bicarbonate of soda and salt into a bowl. Rub in the butter or margarine lightly with your fingertips until the mixture resembles fine breadcrumbs. Stir in the sugar and enough milk to mix to a soft dough.

Turn out the dough on to a floured surface, knead lightly and roll out to a 2 cm (¾ inch) thickness. Cut into 5 cm (2 inch) rounds and place on a floured baking tray. Brush lightly with milk to glaze.

Bake in a preheated oven, 220°C (425°F), Gas Mark 7, for 10 minutes, then transfer to a wire rack to cool. Serve with butter or cream and jam.

Makes about 10

Italian Mocha Cake

150 g (5 oz) butter, softened
1 tablespoon caster sugar
1 tablespoon golden syrup
2 tablespoons cocoa powder
275 g (9 oz) digestive biscuits, finely crushed
25 g (1 oz) ground almonds
2 teaspoons coffee essence
75 g (3 oz) plain chocolate

Grease a shallow 20 cm (8 inch) square tin. Cream the butter and sugar together until pale and fluffy.

Place the syrup in a saucepan and warm gently over a low heat. Remove from the heat and add the cocoa, biscuit crumbs, almonds and coffee essence. Allow to cool and stir into the creamed mixture. Press the mixture into the prepared tin. Cover and chill until firm.

To finish, melt the chocolate, pour evenly over the cake and leave to set. Cut into squares to serve.

Makes about 16

far right: *Italian mocha cake; fruity bars; chocolate fudge bars*

Fruity Bars

175 g (6 oz) dried apricots, finely chopped
50 g (2 oz) seedless raisins, finely chopped
50 g (2 oz) shelled pecan nuts, finely chopped
50 g (2 oz) ground hazelnuts
grated rind of 1 orange
4 teaspoons clear honey
about 4 tablespoons lemon juice
icing sugar, for dusting

Combine the apricots, raisins, pecan nuts, hazelnuts and orange rind in a small bowl. Mix in all the honey and 2 teaspoons of the lemon juice. Stir in the remaining juice gradually until the mixture is a firm paste.

Turn the mixture on to a piece of foil and pat into an oblong shape, about 1.5 cm (¾ inch) thick. Wrap the foil round the mixture to make a flat packet and refrigerate for about 3 hours until firm.

Remove the foil and cut the fruit and nut cake with a sharp knife into small bars, about 7 cm (3 inches) long and 4 cm (1½ inches) wide, or smaller if they are to be served as petit fours. Dust lightly with icing sugar before serving.

Makes about 8

Chocolate Fudge Bars

4 tablespoons golden syrup
125 g (4 oz) butter
125 g (4 oz) plain chocolate, broken into pieces
250 g (8 oz) digestive biscuits, coarsely crushed
50 g (2 oz) desiccated coconut or chopped nuts
50 g (2 oz) glacé cherries, quartered
50 g (2 oz) sultanas

Line the base of an 18 cm (7 inch) square cake tin with some greased greaseproof paper.

Spoon the syrup into a heavy-based saucepan and add the butter. Heat gently until both are melted and stir well. Away from the heat, add the chocolate and then stir vigorously until melted. Stir the biscuit crumbs, coconut or nuts, glacé cherries and sultanas into the chocolate mixture. Mix well.

Pour the mixture into the prepared tin, spreading evenly and pressing down firmly. Cool and then chill in the refrigerator for about 3 hours until set.

Carefully turn out the biscuit slab on to a chopping board and cut into bars. Keep chilled in warm weather.

Makes 15–20

Florentine Slices

250 g (8 oz) block plain chocolate, broken into pieces
50 g (2 oz) butter
125 g (4 oz) demerara sugar
1 egg, beaten
50 g (2 oz) mixed dried fruit
125 g (4 oz) sweetened desiccated coconut
50 g (2 oz) chopped mixed peel or glacé cherries, quartered

Grease a 19 cm (7½ inch) square cake tin. Put the chocolate pieces in a heatproof bowl and place over a pan of hot water until melted, stirring occasionally. Spoon the chocolate into the prepared tin, spreading it out evenly over the bottom, and leave to set.

Meanwhile, cream together the butter and sugar until the mixture is light and fluffy. Beat in the egg thoroughly. Mix together the remaining ingredients and add to the creamed mixture. Spoon into the tin and spread over the set chocolate.

Bake in the centre of a preheated oven, 150°C (300°F), Gas Mark 2, for 40–45 minutes, or until golden brown. Remove from the oven and leave for 5 minutes, then carefully mark into 12–16 squares with a sharp knife. The mixture will be quite sticky at this stage.

Leave until cold, then loosen with a palette knife and lift each square carefully from the tin so as not to mark the chocolate.

Makes 12–16

above: *Florentine slices*
far right: *crunchy muesli bars; coconut-oat chews*

Crunchy Muesli Bars

4 tablespoons vegetable oil
6 tablespoons honey
25 g (1 oz) light muscovado sugar
175 g (6 oz) porridge oats
50 g (2 oz) sunflower seeds
25 g (1 oz) sesame seeds
25 g (1 oz) desiccated coconut
50 g (2 oz) dried apricot pieces, chopped
50 g (2 oz) sultanas

Grease a 28 x 18 cm (11 x 7 inch) baking tin. Put the oil and honey into a saucepan and heat gently until the honey has melted. Remove from the heat and then stir in all the remaining ingredients.

Press the muesli mixture into the prepared tin and level the top. Bake in a preheated oven, 180°C (350°F), Gas Mark 4, for 20–25 minutes until the biscuit is golden brown. Mark it into bars while it is still hot. Cool slightly, then cut into bars. Remove them from the tin and cool on a wire rack.

Makes 16

Coconut-oat Chews

75 g (3 oz) plain flour
125 g (4 oz) caster sugar
50 g (2 oz) desiccated coconut
50 g (2 oz) porridge oats
25 g (1 oz) shelled walnuts, chopped
1 teaspoon bicarbonate of soda
2 tablespoons golden syrup
125 g (4 oz) butter
3 tablespoons water

In a bowl mix together the flour, sugar, coconut, oats, walnuts and bicarbonate of soda.

Put the syrup and butter in a saucepan. Heat until the butter has melted. Add the dry ingredients and water to the pan and mix well.

Shape the mixture into balls, about 2.5 cm (1 inch) across. Place a little apart on greased baking sheets. Bake them in a preheated oven, 180°C (350°F), Gas Mark 4, for 12–15 minutes until golden brown.

Leave on the baking sheets for 2 minutes, and then transfer to a wire rack to cool completely.

Makes about 25

Rock Cakes

50 ml (2 fl oz) boiling water
150 g (5 oz) sultanas or raisins
50 g (2 oz) butter, softened
100 g (3½ oz) soft dark brown sugar
1 egg
25 g (1 oz) shelled walnuts or hazelnuts, chopped
150 g (5 oz) plain flour
½ teaspoon baking powder
½ teaspoon salt
½ teaspoon ground cinnamon

Pour the boiling water over the sultanas or raisins and set aside. Cream together the butter and sugar and beat in the egg. Stir in the nuts. Sift the dry ingredients together and stir into the mixture. Finally, stir in the sultanas or raisins and their liquid and beat well.

Drop the rock cake mixture in heaped teaspoonfuls, spaced about 4 cm (1½ inches) apart, on to lightly greased baking sheets. Bake them in a preheated oven, 180°C (350°F), Gas Mark 4, for about 15–20 minutes until just firm.

Remove the rock cakes from the baking sheets while still warm and cool on a wire rack.

Makes about 20

left: rock cakes; sponge finger biscuits; cocoa wafers

Sponge Finger Biscuits

3 eggs, separated
75 g (3 oz) caster sugar
100 g (3½ oz) plain flour, sifted
2 drops of vanilla essence
sifted icing sugar, for dusting

Line 2 baking sheets with lightly greased greaseproof paper and set aside. Place the egg yolks and sugar in a bowl and beat together until thick and pale in colour.

Beat the egg whites until stiff and fold into the yolk mixture together with the sifted flour and vanilla essence. Spoon the mixture into a piping bag which has been fitted with a 1 cm (½ inch) plain nozzle. Pipe finger lengths of the mixture onto the greaseproof paper.

Dust with sifted icing sugar and bake in a preheated oven, 180°C (350°F), Gas Mark 4, for 10–12 minutes. When cooked, carefully remove the sponge finger biscuits from the paper and leave to cool on a wire rack.

Makes 20

Variation: When completely cold, the ends of the biscuits may be dipped into some melted chocolate.

Cocoa Wafers

125 g (4 oz) unsalted butter, softened
175 g (6 oz) caster sugar
1 egg yolk
1 tablespoon strong black coffee
50 g (2 oz) cocoa powder
125 g (4 oz) plain flour
1 teaspoon baking powder
pinch of salt

Beat the butter in a mixing bowl until pale and soft. Add 150 g (5 oz) of the sugar and beat together until light and fluffy. Beat in the egg yolk and coffee and mix well. Sift the cocoa powder, flour, baking powder and salt into the bowl and mix in until just incorporated.

Shape the dough into a roll 6 cm (2½ inches) in diameter. Wrap the roll in some greaseproof paper and chill in the refrigerator for 2 hours or until firm.

Cut the chilled dough into slices, about 3 mm (⅛ inch) thick, and place on ungreased baking sheets. Lightly sprinkle each 'wafer' with the remaining sugar, pressing it in gently.

Bake in a preheated oven, 200°C (400°F), Gas Mark 6, for 6–8 minutes, until the outside of the wafers just darkens. Remove to a wire rack to cool.

Makes about 40

Peanut Biscuits

300 g (10 oz) plain flour
½ teaspoon baking powder
½ teaspoon salt
½ teaspoon bicarbonate of soda
125 g (4 oz) butter, softened
250 g (8 oz) soft light brown sugar
125 g (4 oz) crunchy peanut butter
2 eggs, beaten

Sift the flour, baking powder, salt and bicarbonate of soda into a bowl. Add the butter, cut into small pieces, and rub into the flour with your fingertips until the mixture resembles fine breadcrumbs. Stir in the sugar. Add the peanut butter and beaten eggs and then mix to a soft dough.

Form the dough into small balls, about 2.5 cm (1 inch) across, and place a little apart on greased baking sheets. Mark each biscuit by pressing the surface with a fork to make a criss-cross pattern.

Bake in a preheated oven, 200°C (400°F), Gas Mark 6, for 12–15 minutes until risen. Remove from the oven and leave for 1 minute, then transfer to a wire rack.

Makes about 50

right: macaroons; peanut biscuits; spiced sultana biscuits

Spiced Sultana Biscuits

250 g (8 oz) self-raising flour
1 teaspoon ground mixed spice
pinch of salt
125 g (4 oz) wholemeal flour
125 g (4 oz) demerara sugar
150 g (5 oz) butter, diced
1 egg, beaten
50 g (2 oz) sultanas
demerara sugar, for sprinkling

Sift the self-raising flour, mixed spice and salt into a bowl. Stir in the wholemeal flour and the sugar. Rub in the diced butter with your fingertips, and then stir in the egg to give a stiff dough.

Turn out the dough on to a floured surface and work in the sultanas with your fingertips until evenly distributed throughout the dough. Sprinkle with more flour if the dough becomes too sticky. Form the dough into a ball, wrap in foil and chill in the refrigerator for at least 30 minutes until firm.

Roll out small pieces of the chilled dough on a floured surface, then cut into rounds, using a 5 cm (2 inch) fluted biscuit cutter. Sprinkle the dough and surface lightly with a little flour while rolling and cutting as the dough is quite rich and sticky.

Place the rounds of dough on some greased baking sheets, prick all over with a fork and sprinkle with demerara sugar. Bake in a preheated oven, 180°C (350°F), Gas Mark 4, for 10–12 minutes until golden brown and set. Transfer immediately to a wire rack and leave to cool.

Makes 30–35

Macaroons

125 g (4 oz) ground almonds
125 g (4 oz) caster sugar
2 egg whites
½ teaspoon almond essence
rice paper, for lining
10 shelled almonds

Mix together the ground almonds and sugar. Whisk the egg whites until stiff in a clean, dry bowl. Fold the ground almond mixture and almond essence into the egg whites.

Spoon the almond mixture into a piping bag which has been fitted with a large plain tube. Pipe 10 rounds, about 5 cm (2 inches) across, on to a baking sheet lined with rice paper. Press an almond into the centre of each macaroon. Bake the macaroons in a medium preheated oven, 180°C (350°F), Gas Mark 4, for about 20–25 minutes until lightly browned and firm. Remove and cool on a wire rack, then trim off the extra rice paper.

Makes 10

Pinwheels

125 g (4 oz) unsalted butter, softened
125 g (4 oz) vanilla sugar
1 teaspoon grated lemon rind
1 egg
200 g (7 oz) plain flour
50 g (2 oz) ground walnuts
½ teaspoon baking powder
pinch of salt
1 tablespoon cocoa powder

Beat the butter in a mixing bowl until pale and soft. Add the sugar and lemon rind and beat until light and fluffy. Beat in the egg. Sift together the flour, walnuts, baking powder and salt into the bowl and fold into the butter mixture.

Halve the dough and set one half aside. Sift the cocoa powder into the bowl with the remaining dough and mix well. Wrap each portion of dough in greaseproof paper and chill in the refrigerator for 1 hour or until firm enough to roll.

Roll out each portion of dough into rectangles of equal size 5 mm (¼ inch) thick. Place one rectangle on top of the other and press gently to seal together. Trim away any uneven sides and roll up the dough from a long side like a Swiss roll. Wrap the roll in greaseproof paper and chill for 2 hours or until firm enough to slice.

Cut the dough into slices, 8 mm (⅓ inch) thick, and place them on buttered baking sheets. Bake in a preheated oven, 200°C (400°F), Gas Mark 6, for 8–10 minutes, until the edges are crisp. Remove to a wire rack to cool.

Makes 30

Langues de Chats

125 ml (4 fl oz) double cream
125 g (4 oz) icing sugar, sifted
125 g (4 oz) plain flour, sifted
2 egg whites
finely grated rind of 1 lemon

Place the cream and icing sugar in a bowl and stir together. Add the flour and stir in lightly. Whisk the egg whites in a clean, dry bowl until stiff and standing in peaks. Fold one-third of the egg white into the mixture at a time. Add the lemon rind and lightly mix until evenly blended.

Put the mixture into a piping bag fitted with a 5 mm (¼ inch) or 1 cm (½ inch) plain nozzle and then pipe in finger lengths on to a greased baking sheet.

As each baking sheet is filled, bake in a preheated oven, 190°C (375°F), Gas Mark 5, for about 7–8 minutes until the biscuits are golden brown round the edges but still pale in the centre. Cool the biscuits on a wire rack.

Makes 50 small or 20 large biscuits

Citrus Almond Galettes

65 g (2½ oz) butter, softened
100 g (3½ oz) caster sugar
75 g (3 oz) blanched almonds, chopped
75 g (3 oz) candied orange peel, chopped
40 g (1½ oz) plain flour, sifted
2 teaspoons milk

Cream the butter and sugar together until light and fluffy. Stir in the almonds and candied orange peel, then the flour and milk.

Place the almond mixture in small spoonfuls, 5 cm (2 inches) apart, on a lightly greased baking sheet. Flatten each spoonful gently with a wet fork.

Bake the galettes in a preheated oven, 220°C (425°F), Gas Mark 7, for 3–4 minutes before removing to a wire rack to cool.

Makes 18–20

far left: *pinwheels*
left: *langues de chats; citrus almond galettes*

Oat Biscuits

125 g (4 oz) plain flour
½ teaspoon salt
125 g (4 oz) rolled oats
50 g (2 oz) caster sugar
65 g (2½ oz) lard or margarine
1 egg, beaten
2–3 tablespoons milk

Sift the flour and salt into a mixing bowl. Mix in the rolled oats and sugar. Cut the fat into the mixture, then rub in with your fingertips until the mixture resembles fine breadcrumbs. Bind with the beaten egg, adding milk as necessary to make a stiff dough.

Roll out the dough thinly on a floured board. With a plain cutter, cut out 6 cm (2½ inch) rounds. Place on a greased baking sheet.

Bake in a preheated oven, 180°C (350°F), Gas Mark 4, for 15 minutes or until crisp and golden. Cool the biscuits on a wire tray.

Makes about 24

far right: *oat biscuits; Cornish fairings; chocolate rings*

Cornish Fairings

These little biscuits were sold at the fairs which were held all over the West Country. There are several kinds but these are the crunchy Cornish variety.

250 g (8 oz) self-raising flour
1½ teaspoons bicarbonate of soda
pinch of salt
1 teaspoon ground ginger
1 teaspoon mixed spice
½ teaspoon ground cinnamon
125 g (4 oz) butter or margarine
50 g (2 oz) caster sugar
125 g (4 oz) golden syrup

Sift the flour, bicarbonate of soda, salt and spices into a bowl. Rub in the butter with the fingertips until the mixture resembles breadcrumbs. Stir in the sugar. Heat the golden syrup a little, and then pour it into the bowl and knead until it forms a firm dough.

Flour your hands and roll the dough into small balls. Arrange them on a greased baking sheet, well spaced out. Flatten down well with the back of a spoon.

Bake in the centre of a preheated oven, 190°C (375°F), Gas Mark 5, for about 10 minutes or until golden brown. Remove the fairings from the baking sheet and cool on a wire tray.

Makes about 30

Chocolate Rings

125 g (4 oz) butter, at room temperature
125 g (4 oz) caster sugar
1 egg, beaten
drop of vanilla essence
250 g (8 oz) plain flour
25 g (1 oz) cocoa powder
2 x 25 g (1 oz) chocolate flakes
175 g (6 oz) plain chocolate

Cream the butter and sugar until pale and fluffy. Beat in the egg and vanilla essence. Sift the flour and cocoa together and stir into the mixture. Add the crushed flakes.

Turn out on to a floured surface and knead lightly to a smooth dough. Wrap in clingfilm and chill in the refrigerator for 30 minutes.

Roll out the chocolate dough to about 5 mm (¼ inch) thick on a floured surface, then cut into 5 cm (2 inch) rounds with a plain cutter. Remove the centres with a smaller cutter and place the rings on a lightly greased baking sheet.

Bake in a preheated oven, 190°C (375°F), Gas Mark 5, for 15 minutes. After 2 minutes, remove from the baking tray and cool on a wire rack.

Melt the chocolate gently in a small bowl over a pan of hot water. When the biscuits are cold, dip the top of each ring, holding it on a fork, into the melted chocolate and then place on a sheet of oiled greaseproof paper and leave to set.

Makes about 24

Index